The IMPACT

Upon Secondary Victims

Charles M. Ridulph

BALBOA
PRESS
A DIVISION OF HAY HOUSE

Balboa Press books may be ordered through booksellers or by contacting:

Balboa Press
A Division of Hay House
1663 Liberty Drive
Bloomington, IN 47403
www.balboapress.com
1 (877) 407-4847

Because of the dynamic nature of the Internet, any web addresses or links contained in this book may have changed since publication and may no longer be valid. The views expressed in this work are solely those of the author and do not necessarily reflect the views of the publisher, and the publisher hereby disclaims any responsibility for them.

The author of this book does not dispense medical advice or prescribe the use of any technique as a form of treatment for physical, emotional, or medical problems without the advice of a physician, either directly or indirectly. The intent of the author is only to offer information of a general nature to help you in your quest for emotional and spiritual well-being. In the event you use any of the information in this book for yourself, which is your constitutional right, the author and the publisher assume no responsibility for your actions.

Any people depicted in stock imagery provided by Thinkstock are models, and such images are being used for illustrative purposes only. Certain stock imagery © Thinkstock.

Print information available on the last page.

ISBN: 978-1-5043-6454-6 (sc)
ISBN: 978-1-5043-6455-3 (hc)
ISBN: 978-1-5043-6457-7 (e)

Library of Congress Control Number: 2016913169

Balboa Press rev. date: 09/20/2016

Cover
By
McKenzie Rae Palm

In Memory of
Maria Elizabeth Ridulph

Dedicated to
My sister Pat
and
My loving wife Diane

Contents

The Introduction

Many of us, if not all, have experienced some tragedy in our lives. Yes, the Bible tells us very clearly that *In this world you will have trouble. John 16:33.* And I mean real trouble, real tragedy! But, Jesus goes on to say, *I have overcome the world.*

As I look at my life, I don't see it as filled or dominated by tragedy even though some see it differently. You know the world looks at things differently than we as Christians do. An old friend and classmate from Concordia College has told me on several occasions that he has used my life as an example for others. After prep-school for the ministry he decided to go into the medical field. He would tell my story to patients to show that not all is hopeless and lost. Each time I hear it I am not sure as to whether I should take it as a compliment or not. But it certainly is true. Our lives should not be defined by the tragedies that we live through. I almost wrote here that our lives are not defined by the tragedies, but quickly realized that is not always the case. Sometimes we allow the tragedy to define who we are.

Over the past several years it has been suggested to me that I should write a book about my life. I must admit that I had thought of writing a book about my ministry to seniors and those with special needs, however, I never considered my life as something of interest to others. And that thinking has not changed. *The Impact* is not so much about my life, but about how God intervened so that my life would be defined by his grace rather than the world's tragedies.

On May 7, 2015, Deaconess Jana Peters, a ministry consultant with Bethesda Lutheran Communities, contacted me. She asked if I might meet with her concerning ways the Bethesda staff could support employees who were dealing with death by murder. I had been recommended to her as a possible resource by one of our sister-congregation's Lutheran Church Missouri Synod pastors. I was recommended because of my experience with the kidnapping, rape, and murder of my seven year old sister Maria. After our meeting Jana thanked me for my insight into the many emotions which we as victims of violent crime experience and need to deal with. She also suggested that I consider writing prayers and lessons for each level or stage of this process. I thought the suggestion was good and it went into one of my many pending, or to do later file folders.

On December 10, 2015, Deaconess Peters again called. She at this time was convinced of a larger, wider-spread need for guidance and consoling for those suffering from the effects of violent crime. She wondered if I would be willing to help in exploring ways in which we might be able to provide some consoling for those victims of some violent tragedy in their lives. I told her that I would certainly be willing to participate in that discussion. As of today, we have not moved forward with such a program, however, this is the conversation which led me to seriously consider the writing of *The Impact*.

In *The Impact* I tell of the areas which needed to be addressed in my life after the tragic kidnapping and murder of my sister. Many victims of violent crime may not even realize how deeply and completely they have been impacted. Many emotions; many stages of grief do not raise their ugly head for days, weeks, and even years. But when they do it can be overwhelming. It is my prayer, that as I share how God has led me through the valley of the shadow of death; as I share how God has shown me that my cup runneth over even in the aftermath of tragedy, that you also will find the peace and joy which is ours in Christ Jesus our Lord.

Chapter One

The Time Before

My name is Charles Michael Ridulph. I was born on February 11, 1946, in the typical small mid-western town of Sycamore, Illinois. World War II had ended, and I was among the first group of children who came to be known as the *Baby Boomers*. A normal family in a normal small town. My father had immigrated to the United States from Italy when he was nine years old and my mother was a first-generation American of Swiss and German descent. I had three sisters: Patricia (Pat) who was five years older than me; Kay who was four years older; and Maria who was four years younger.

Growing up at the time and in the place where I grew up was the next best thing to perfect; if there is such a thing. It was just after the war, a time when it seemed we had everything we could possibly want; a time of contentment so to speak. Unemployment, although there must have been some, was not an issue. We had electricity, although some in the rural areas (which by the way were within walking distance) was provided via a windmill. We had running water, except again, in some rural areas where it had to be brought into the home from the pump next to the windmill. Most of us had telephones, the kind connected to the wall by a wire; the kind in which you needed the aid of an operator (a real person) to connect you to any person outside of your immediate area. But most of us had telephones which used what we called *party lines*. Party lines were phones that used the same line. In other words, when you wanted to make a call you first had to pick-up the phone and listen to make sure someone was not already using the line. I think private lines were available for an extra charge, but during those days most people were not willing to pay extra for anything that would have been considered an unnecessary extravagance. At my house we were very lucky. We shared the line with the Johnsons across the street and they almost never used the phone. It was like having a private line but without the extravagant extra cost.

Now, television on the other hand was something different. It was considered somewhat of an extravagance. Well, maybe extravagance is really not the word to be used here, because in the early fifties black and white television sets had become fairly common household items. We had four channels. I think. And at midnight (or maybe before on some channels) *The Star Spangled Banner* was played and they went off the air. We had it all!

My father, who had an eighth grade education, worked as a machinist at the Diamond Wire and Cable Company just a few blocks from our house. At that time Sycamore offered a large variety of opportunities for employment at their many local manufacturing plants. Nearly all Sycamore residents worked locally, and there was company as well as employee loyalty. The factories and employees became an extended family. There were factory picnics and Christmas parties; and I mean real PICNICS...with loads of food, unlimited pop and ice cream, clowns, fire engine and pony rides, softball games, horseshoes, sack races, and egg tosses, and of course bingo. And CHRISTMAS PARTIES...real Christmas parties with a tree and carols; with food, drink, and an assortment of cookies. There would be a Santa and a gift for each of the kids along with a turkey for each of the families. The factories provided summer swimming pool passes. They sponsored sports teams, everything from Little League baseball to mixed adult bowling leagues. The family, not just the employee, was important to the company.

My mother came to Illinois from a farm in Iowa so she could attended Joliet Junior College. She later met my father in her small breakfast and lunch diner which she had built in downtown Sycamore. After their marriage they ran the restaurant together until it was sold so that she could spend her time raising their children. Nearly all of my memories of my mother as a child were of her being a stay-at-home mom.

We lived in what today would be considered a very small house, especially for a family of six. It was a seven room house with one full and one half bath. It had a full basement with a one car garage. At the time I was growing up it did not seem small, even though I shared a bedroom with my little sister Maria. We had a nice yard with the back fenced in, and of course a large garden; large enough to furnish nearly all of our vegetables for the entire year. We also had a peach tree which provided only a few peaches every other year, and yet was my father's pride and joy. We had an apple tree and a pear tree which provided what seemed to be an endless supply of fruit, and our neighbor had a cherry tree which was loaded with cherries each year. It was a harvest which they did not appreciate, so we adopted that tree and its bounty for our own. I still remember the tedious job, which seemed to always be mine, of pitting all those cherries. One by one each cherry was placed into this primitive spring loaded punch which was mounted on the lid of a quart mason jar. This device when pushed would punch the cherry pit through the cherry and through a hole in the lid into the jar. Then you would brush the pitted cherry into a bowl and repeat the process…over, and over again.

The fruits and vegetables which were not grown and harvested at home were gotten fresh elsewhere. Sweet corn and lima beans were available from our local canning factory. Asparagus was found in abundance growing wild along the railroad tracks, and berries of all sorts could be picked at local commercial farms. It was a great deal of work, preparing, canning, and freezing all this produce, but boy was it worth it. And, a bonus; it was a family affair. I remember vividly all of us out in those strawberry patches picking berries, and perhaps eating at times more than we picked along the way. I remember it as a fun thing to do; not as a chore. Yes. We grew up, at least as I like to remember, as a family living, and working, and playing together.

Growing up in Sycamore during the fifties has often been referred to as growing up in *Mayberry, R.F.D.*, and our families being compared to the Cleavers. I would like to think of it that way, and in some ways it definitely was, but I am afraid I must say not that perfect. I loved my early childhood, and I can't say that we wanted for anything. It was sure a lot simpler then; not as many distractions. The police and others in authority were respected. We listened to our teachers, at least for the most part, and we were polite to our elders. Was there any mischief going on around town? You can bet there was. I remember one time we found an old life-sized mannequin in an alley behind Anderson Brothers clothing store. We dressed it up with some old clothes and a hat we found around the house. We then put it on roller-skates and attached a rope to it. That night after it turned dark, we hid behind a tree and pulled it across the street in front of on-coming cars on Center Cross Street. We were awfully cleaver for just a bunch of neighborhood kids don't you think? But, all-in-all Sycamore was a place where you felt safe and secure.

One thing I can tell you for sure, as a kid growing up in the fifties we knew how to play. And, living in Sycamore, the entire town was our playground. School grounds, back yards, and vacant lots became our arenas. There we played baseball and football. We built boxing rings and platforms for concerts and plays. We played cowboys and Indians, and built igloos and mounds of snow for king-of-the hill. We were in Little League, in Cub Scouts, then Boy Scouts, or Brownies, then Girl Scouts. We rode bikes and walked around with a skate key tied around or necks. There was Ennie-Eye-Over, hide-n-seek, and even Monopoly and Canasta, kick-the-can, and rover-come-over. Yes, Sycamore was our playground.

Was it all fun and games? No. With life here on earth, regardless of the era, there are life's problems. In my house, for as long as I can remember, my mother and my father would fight, and sometimes those fights were knock-down, drag-out. Not always though. Mostly it was calm and quiet. My parents bowled in a league together and belonged to a card club. Other than that they would seldom go out, with the exception of New Year's Eve. New Year's Eve was a big deal around our house, almost like a little Christmas or Easter. On New Year's Day my sisters and I would rush downstairs to claim our choice of hats, lays, and noise makers from the assortment they would bring home from the party they attended. It didn't take much in those days to make a kid happy.

I think it is important to let you know that I did not start here when I began writing this book. The night before I actually started to put something down on paper, when I thought about testing the water to see if I was really going to attempt this, I was lying awake in bed, as I often do, with my mind just wandering. The day before, I had seen Jimmy McMillian at the YMCA. Jimmy was my sister Maria's age and lived down the street from us at the time Maria was kidnapped; in fact he still lives in the same house today. At the trial of Jack McCullough for the murder of my sister Maria, Jimmy was one of many interviewed by the press. He said, "I can't stop thinking that if only I had been with Maria and Kathy that night maybe I could have done something to stop him." That statement just would not leave me. That is where I began in the writing of this book. I began with the chapter on *The Reliving*. At the time I thought it was a little strange not to be starting at the beginning, but now as I write about *The Time Before* I am glad that I did. I am glad because now as I look back to the beginning I see it from a different perspective. I am able to write about the time before with a greater appreciation. I am able to write about the time before from the perspective of the impact of this horrible crime. I am able to write about the time before not only from a historical point of view, but I am able to really appreciate *The Time Before.* Yes, thank God for all the memories of the time before.

Great are the works of the Lord; they are
pondered by all who delight in them.
He has caused his wonders to be remembered.
Psalm 111:2-4

Prayer on remembering the wonders.

Father of all mercies, I come before you today knowing that you are the provider of all good things. And yet, I still so often forget. I often fail to remember your great gifts of the past. I often fail to remember your protective hand which has brought us to today. Father forgive me.

Father of all mercies, I come before you today with a thankful heart as I remember and as I acknowledge how richly I have been blessed. I thank you Father for providing all that I have needed, and so much more. I thank you Father for bringing to memory all the good which you have placed in my life. I thank you Father for bringing to memory your great wonders which overpower any and all difficulties which the world brings.

Father of all mercies, now I would ask that you continue to bless me with your goodness. I ask that you enable me to remember and to see the wonder of your hands and your marvelous works of the past. I ask that you enable me to know with certainty that your wonders will never cease. And I pray all this in Jesus name. Amen.

Next Thursday, February 11, 2016, I will turn seventy years old. The day before yesterday I received a note from my good friend Mark Overby. He began with a quote which read, "We do not remember days; we remember moments." And then he went on to say, "On your 70th birthday, I hope there are many moments that you will always remember. May your day be bright and full of laughter and fun, and the love of family and friends."

This morning I preached on the Transfiguration of Our Lord, a special event in the journey of Christ to the cross. And I began by speaking of crossroads; of different kinds of crossroads at different times of life. And, when you come to a crossroad, you tend to stop for a moment and look around. You look forward to what lies ahead, and to look back at what has come and gone before. This is what I am doing here today. I have come to a crossroad and I am stopping for a moment to look around.

You will be changed into a different person.
1 Samuel 10:6

Prayer on personal change.

Lord of heaven and earth, I bow before you with praise and adoration. You are the ruler of all things, past, present, and future. I bow before you with complete trust, since I have seen your miracles.

But Lord, sometimes I falter. Sometimes I do not remember your miracles. Sometimes I do not anticipate your good and gracious gifts. Sometimes I forget your promises. Lord, please forgive me.

Lord of heaven and earth, I thank you for all your blessings, and I look forward to each new day with anticipation of greater things to come. I know of the victory which is mine in Christ Jesus, and I know of your great love for me. Lord, I thank you today especially for the family and friends which you have placed in my life as a reminder of your goodness.

Lord, as I remember the past, and as I come to the crossroads of the present and of the future, enable me to stop for a moment and look around. Enable me to change. Enable me to be more Christ like. Oh Lord, enable me to be uplifted and guided by your might and your power, for I have indeed seen your great love. In Christ Jesus. Amen.

The Ridulph family vacations were modest, but we always looked forward to them, and we always took one. No Cruises or anything like that. But usually a week in a cabin on Lake Ripley, Wisconsin, and then a week in Iowa to stay with Mom's family on the farm. You know, as I look back on this time, I see that my early childhood in Sycamore was like one long vacation, and these special summer trips were simply a part of it.

Cousin Gigi, Maria, Aunt Josephine, sister Pat, sister Kay,
and Chuck on vacation at Lake Ripley, Wisconsin.

Life in the fifties was different than now. It was certainly slower, and as I think about it, I would say it was also more structured. There seemed to be set times and days for nearly everything. Not so many options as there are today; not so many conflicts, and more absolutes. Have you ever heard the phrase, "The family that eats together stays together." Or, even "The family that prays together stays together." Or, "The family that plays together stays together." Sounds so simple doesn't it? And, you know what? It was simple.

In our house we were active, and I mean active as a family. My mother was a Cub Scout pack leader for me, and a Brownie leader for my sisters. My father was active with me in the Boy Scouts, and coached me throughout baseball Future, Little, and Pony leagues. We would hunt and fish together, and our friends were always welcome in our home. And, you know what? I don't ever remember fighting with my sisters over anything. Never! As I write that down on paper even I find it hard to believe. My parents fought. Boy, did they fight. But, I never recall fighting with my sisters.

My father and I spent a great deal of time together. I would help him with the yard work, especially with the gardening. He was always helping me in making things. I was the only kid around with a home-made kite, and boy would it fly. We would take it across the street to the West School yard and on just the right day we could put that kite up so high that we could just barely see it as a speck in the sky. We would tie it to the fence and go home for lunch returning later to start the process of rolling that nylon string around a stick in order to bring that kite back down.

We had all kinds of pets, which over the years, beginning with Pat, then Kay, then me, and finally Maria, made their way to show-n-tell, at first to the "old" West School house and then to the "new". There they went: a dog named Mitzi; a cat named Puffy; then rabbits, pigeons, fish, and an occasional hamster or a frog. I started hunting with my dad at about the age of six, and got my first 410 shotgun for Christmas when I was eight. We would go fishing at every opportunity and it didn't really matter if we caught anything. Many a late summer afternoon was spent in the back yard where my dad would give me batting practice by pitching to me the apples which had fallen from the tree. Yes. My life as a kid was good.

My father was a Roman Catholic from childhood although not practicing as an adult. (He later became a confirmed member of the Lutheran Church Missouri Synod shortly after I started study for the ministry) My mother was a very active member of St. John Lutheran Church in Sycamore, a Missouri Synod congregation. She sang in the choir and was a member of the Ladies Aid. Church, our faith, was an important part of our lives. I grew up in a family where our Christian faith always played an important role. In fact, there was never a time in my life in which I did not believe in Jesus Christ. I grew up in an era in which for most Christian children church or Sunday school was not an option. We were not asked if we wanted to go to Sunday school, it was just a given that we would go. Even when going on vacation we would go to Sunday school always getting a signed confirmation that we had attended since we did not want anything to interfere with our perfect attendance. And it might be a surprise to many today, but this is not simply something which our parents wanted for us, but something which we as children wanted. Yes. The perfect attendance Sunday school pin was very important and we wore them proudly. All of us had them: Pat, Kay, myself, and Maria. All of us had perfect attendance in Sunday school.

Chuck and Maria proudly wearing their perfect
attendance Sunday school pins.

In the 1950's era being a Christian was not something that you would be ashamed of or hide. The church was not only important to the individual or to the family, but also to the community. The churches and the schools worked together. The public school system did not attempt to block out all reference to God trying to pretend that he did not exist. The school did not ridicule a Christian child for their beliefs. In fact, the public school system in our community even set aside a day of the week in which they would not schedule any school activities, reserving Wednesday as *Church Activity Day*. Very different from today don't you think? Today, when the church is under attack from all directions, including the public schools. And so I, along with my sisters, would spend Wednesday afternoons and even some evenings in church activities such as choir and confirmation class. Yes. Our church and our faith were important to us. The Church had a prominent place in our lives and in our community.

As a child I never felt alone. It was a time in which you knew your neighbor and you trusted them. I would run errands for them, mow their lawns, shovel their snow, and play in their yards. If I fell down or out of a tree, they would run to my aid, and bring me in and bandage my knee. I certainly did not fear my neighbor.

When you neighbor became sick, or there was a death in the family, the entire neighborhood would come to their aid. Dinners were prepared. The clergy would call. Children would be cared for. Their homes would be watched over. Love would be shared.

Jesus said, "Love your neighbor as yourself".
Matthew 19:19

Jesus said, "You have heard that it was said, 'Love
you neighbor and hate your enemy'.
But I tell you: Love your enemies and pray for those who persecute you."
Mathew 5:43

Pray for our neighbor and our enemies.

O God of love and grace, you are the great enabler; you have shown me what love truly is. And yet, I often do not, or cannot, love as you have loved me. Forgive me Lord for I am all too often concerned only for myself. Help me O Lord to recognize my neighbor. Help me to appreciate them, to see them as you see them, to love them. Enable me oh God of love and grace, to love my neighbor as you have loved me.

I thank you oh God of love and grace, for the love and the encouragement I have received from the neighbors you have placed in my path. I pray that their actions be an example for me. But Lord, there are also those whom have not been good to me. There are those that have hurt me. There are those that I fear. There are those that I resent. I pray now that you would relieve me of those ill feelings. Enable me to pray for them that your love and grace may touch their lives as it has touched mine. In Jesus name. Amen.

On December 3, 1957, my life was changed forever. I was eleven years old.

Lord, teach us to pray.
Luke 11:1

Chapter Two

The Events Unfold

The reliving of this terrible time in my life has taken many forms throughout the years and I am sure that there will be more to come as there will be for you as well. You see, the impact is far reaching, and the impact, the reliving, is different and yet the same for all of us. And the reliving of tragedy affects us differently at different times in our lives.

At the time of the tragedy we are simply overwhelmed. Our minds are racing as we try to understand what is happening, and at the same time we are numb. We go over and over what is happening trying to understand, but at the same time trying to convince ourselves that it is not what it seems to be. There is so much commotion, real commotion and activity going on all around us, and real commotion going on within our minds. Questions are being thrown at you from all sides; questions which you are answering out of a state of confusion. You are in a deep fog. Your mind is filled with questions of your own. You just don't know where to turn. You are thinking, "What was I doing?" and now, "What should I be doing?" You are thinking, "What time was it when she went out?" and then, "Why did I let her go out?" And even now, as I am writing this, a question pops into my mind which never did before: "Why didn't I go out looking for her when Kathy first came to the door and said that she couldn't find my sister?" This new question is something which might have haunted me back then, but thank God it will not today.

There are things which happened, or did not happen, at the time of the tragedy which may plague you for a lifetime. That in and of itself would be another tragedy. Many times you as a loved one may look back and exclaim, "Oh No! The last time I saw her I yelled at her." Or, "The last time I saw her she asked me for some help and I ignored her because I was too busy." I thank God that I did not have to experience this. All my memories then and now of my sister Maria are good ones. But, this type of thinking belongs with the *What if's*. This type of thinking can serve no other purpose but to torment. As soon as those thoughts come into your mind they must be discarded.

Avoid it, do not travel on it; turn from it and go on your way.
Proverbs 4:15

Prayer on thinking.

Almighty God, Ruler over all things, I need you today to rule over my mind. Saint Paul has told us in so many ways that we are to fill our minds with good thoughts leaving no room for that which is bad. And yet I am plagued with troubling thoughts and questions. I am confused, and the Devil is using my confusion against me. I pray oh Lord that you enable me by the power of your Holy Spirit to heed your warning to "Avoid it, do not travel on it; turn from it and go on my way." Yes, Almighty God, Ruler over all things, fill my mind with good thoughts, leaving no room for that which is bad. Amen.

At the time of the tragedy you are in somewhat of a state of disbelief. But as the events unfold there comes the point where reality sets in. For me, when that point came, it was a shock. My seven year old sister was missing, or should I say at that point our thinking was that she simply could not be found, and I went looking. I went searching the immediate neighborhood not even thinking that she might not be found. But with that being said, looking back and retracing my steps, I recall something. As I walked around our block looking for Maria a police car drove by and at that moment I thought that maybe I should have stopped it and asked for help. I did not.

When I returned home empty handed, our concerns were escalating. Kathy had told us that when she left Maria on the corner to go home for her mittens there was a man with her. We went out searching and calling again, but this time more intently. I was looking in back yards and behind garages. As I looked between the fence and a garage near the corner where the girls were playing, I saw this figure in the dark which turned out to be a small bush. It scared me. It scared me because in that instant I realized what I was looking for. The reality of what was unfolding was beginning to sink in. I went home.

Now the possibility of Maria being kidnapped was quickly becoming real. Our hearts and our minds were filled with panic. I sit here now, and as I look back at those first minutes, hours, and days of looking for Maria, I feel as empty as I did then. We all wanted to just make it better. We all wanted a happy ending, but at the same time feared the worst. And the entire community and beyond joined us in our search, that search for Maria's safe return. And as the days went by, as we struggled with uncertainty, we continued to hope. We prayed. We waited.

Wait for the Lord; be strong and take heart and wait for the Lord.
Psalm 27:14

Prayer on waiting for the Lord.

O Lord, my God, you are indeed Lord of all, and I rejoice in that certainty. You are my Rock and my Salvation, and in that I trust. But I must confess that I am weak, and often impatient. I say that I trust you, but where is my trust? Forgive me oh Lord. Forgive me and renew me.

You have shown me time and time again your great strength, and I thank you for that. You have provided me with all the evidence necessary to know that no matter how difficult my situation may be, that you will deliver me. Help me to hold on to that certainty. Help me to grasp hold of your strength. Help me oh Lord, to wait; to wait in the sure hope that you will lift me up. Amen.

The night my sister Maria was kidnapped is forever etched in my mind. It is as though I have been picked up and placed back in time. I see myself standing there in the midst of it all, but it is as though no one can see me. It is funny. I can remember it so well. I remember every knock on the door. But the snow, that light snow which invited Maria and Kathy to go out and play that night, that snow I don't remember. I saw it. I walked in it. I touched it. But I don't remember it. The beauty of the snow escaped me. It was overshadowed by the evil which was unfolding.

Now the stage is set. Which part will we play? Will we be swept up by the evil that is swirling around us, or will we turn to God? Is it this evil act that will define us, or will we prevail in spite of it? At the moment, on that night of December 3, 1957, our minds were overloaded with emotions. But most of all our minds were filled with fear, and fear can be crippling. There was so much confusion; people everywhere. But in the center of it all, I remember Reverend Going, our pastor at St. John Lutheran Church. In the center of it all, there was prayer; private prayer and public prayer. We were praying. The Church was praying. The community was praying, and soon people around the world would be praying. Yes. The stage was set, and God was at the center.

Turn to the Lord your God with all your heart and with all your soul.
Deuteronomy 30:10

Prayer on turning to the Lord.

Unto thee, O Lord, I turn. You are the source and the center of all things. You are the ruler of all creation, and to you I turn, and I must turn with all my heart, and with all my soul. But I must confess O Lord, that I do not always do so. Forgive me Lord, and enable me by the power of the Holy Spirit to come to you in true confidence that you are indeed Lord over all things.

O Lord, I thank you for all of your intercessions of the past, and I thank you for all of your promises for the present, and even more so for the future. And now I ask that you not let me be swept up by the evil which swirls around me. I ask that my prayers be not only heard, but answered to my benefit and to your great glory. Amen.

As I look back over my life I can see a definite pattern. All of us go through stages. We all go through periods of time when we are near to God, and periods when we move away from him. Sometimes these periods of time are brief as our walk with God fluctuates throughout any given day or even any given hour. Sometimes these periods of time are significant.

Recently I preached on how Jesus wept over how the children of God had strayed. Jesus told the people of how he longed to gather the children together as a hen gathers her chicks under her wings, but they were not willing! I told of how wild animals and even domestic pets seem to know more than we do. I told of how by nature these other animals stay close to their protectors, close to food and shelter. Just as Jesus used the example of chicks not straying far from the protection of the hen's wings. I explained how this was simply the natural order, the instinct of survival, given by God. Animals stay close to the one that nurtures and protects them.

I then asked, but what about you? What about people? You see, that's another story. We, you and I, are the only ones that stray. Yes. We are the only creatures that exhibit the unnatural behavior of turning away from the love and protection of the God that made us, and he longs to bring us back. He longs to protect us. He longs to provide all that we need.

God loves us. God loves you. And yet, says Jesus, we have strayed. We have wandered, we have removed ourselves from his presence. But Jesus now tells us that as a mother hen spreads her wings over her brood, so God would spread protective wings over us. That is what he wants for us. However it appears that is not what we want. How foolish. How unnatural. What chicks would not do, could not do, we so often have done. In essence you and I count the love and protection of God as nothing, choosing instead to go our own way.

I went on to ask, how could such a thing be? How could the children of Israel, how could you and I be so foolish? Especially when God had delivered them time and time again from their enemies. We have seen the history of it all, and yet, we do not have to go back into history to see what God has done. I have seen it in my own life over and over again. And yet I often continue to stray from the protecting wings of God.

Well, let me ask you, are you any different? Can you say that you are trouble free; that you can take care of yourself? How are you dealing with the darkness, the tragedy, the sickness, the evil which seems to come your way all too often? We have seen the tragedy. We have felt its blow. And yet we at times do not hear our Lord as he calls to us. We stray. We make the unnatural choices. It is like a commercial I saw on television not too long ago where these kids are running from the chain-saw murderer. One says, "Let's get in that running car." Another says, "Are you crazy? Let's run into the cemetery." Well, what about us? Are we crazy? Where do we place our trust? Where do we turn with our worries, our pain, and our emptiness?

God calls to us. God offers, he pledges to us, all that he has. And one of the great things is that we do not have to search him out. We do not have to wonder where to go. He is there; right now and forever. He this there, with his arms outstretched, as a hen with her wings gathering her chicks.

They refused to listen and failed to remember the
miracles you performed among them...
You did not desert them...Because of your great compassion
You did not abandon them in the desert.
Nehemiah 9:17,19

Prayer on remaining close to God.

O Lord, my Guide and my Protector, I have often turned away from you. I have often failed to remember your might, your power, and your great love. Forgive me Lord.

O Lord, my Guide and my Protector, I thank you for your call to me; your assurance that you have not forsaken me. Enable me, O Lord, in this dark hour, to see your face and hear your voice. Enable me, O Lord, to accept your invitation to come to you for comfort, guidance, protection, and deliverance. Amen.

The events which were unfolding before my eyes would forever leave their mark upon me. The evil which was invading my life could become such an effective instrument of the Devil as he is always prowling and searching for ways to snatch us out of God's hand. Now, in the midst of such confusion, uncertainty, and fear, where would I go? Would I be listening to my pain, or would I be listening to the call of my Lord? Would I be walking in the shadow of darkness, or would I be drawn by the light and the love of Jesus my Savior?

As I look back over my life, if I were to draw a chart or a graph of the good and peaceful times, or the high-points of my life, and also of the low points, and then draw a separate graph of the times in my life when I was near to God and walking with him, along with the times when I was not, I would see that they were the same. If I were to place one graph over the other the highs and the lows would match up.

Now, don't get confused. Do not misunderstand. I am not suggesting that just because you are walking with God in Christ Jesus that your life will be trouble or pain free. But what I am saying is that when that trouble, when and if that tragedy does strike, the impact, the pain will be real, but it will be different.

Before I wrote those four words *it will be different*, I sat here for several minutes trying to find better words to express what I am saying. The words escape me. But as I think about it, that is OK. You see, God simply has a way of changing things! That is who he is, and that is what he does. God changes things. Yes. God changes things, and because God is love, because God is all that is good, you can be certain that he will change things for the better. Yes, tragedy brings with it pain and suffering, but with God it will be different.

> *The Spirit of the Lord will come upon you in power...*
> *And you will be changed into a different person.*
> *1 Samuel 10:6*

Prayer on walking with God changes things.

O Father of mercies and God of all comfort, I know in my mind who you are. I say with my lips what you can and will do, but I must confess that I do not always rely totally upon the certainty of your mercy and your comfort. Therefore I pray that the Holy Spirit will come upon me in power. I pray that you will change, if not the horrible circumstances which surround me, then you change me so that I can see beyond them. Yes, Father of mercies and God of all comfort, change me; shape me so that I may grasp your mercies and your comfort. Change me and shape me so that my path may be altered. I pray all this in confidence in the name of Christ Jesus. Amen.

The search for Maria intensified and continued through the night. Road blocks were set-up surrounding the town. Yards, cars, garages, and even homes were searched. But nothing turned up. The next day search parties were put together, including men from all over the surrounding area. Men who were released from their places of work. Boy scouts, and high school students who were excused from school, all joining in the search. My father and I joined in. I was assigned to a group which began its search one block from my home going west into the corn fields. The same corn fields I had hunted only a couple of weeks before with my father, an area in which I had shot my first rabbit. Before we reached the corn fields we searched the land surrounding Johnson's Greenhouse which was being developed for new homes. The sewer line was just being put in, and since I was the smallest I was sent down into the man-hole to search. It was awful thinking about what I was looking for, searching and yet hoping not to discover anything.

The searches continued, and we as a family went through the motions of living. My father returned to work, and my sisters and I went back to school. We were different now, and we were treated differently. We were the victims of a horrible, evil crime. And we did not even know to what extent. Maria was lost, and so were we.

There were extensive searches organized throughout
Sycamore and the surrounding area.

And this is the will of him who sent me; that I shall
lose none of all that he has given me.
John 6:39

Prayer: We are not lost.

Gracious Father, Caretaker of my soul and Protector of my life, I have felt alone and lost, and I have searched. I feared that Maria was alone and lost, and I cried. I forgot the promise of my Savior that he would not lose those that you have given him. Let me, O Gracious Father, find strength and comfort in those words. Let me know that I am not lost. But most of all let me rejoice in the midst of my sorrow that Maria is not lost. Let me find strength and comfort in the fact that we are safe in the arms of our Lord and Savior. Amen.

Looking back over time, as the events unfolded, as the confusion turned into reality, as our worst fears became more and more a strong possibility, I had this empty feeling. As we as a family went through the motions of our daily lives, as best as was possible under the circumstances, I can only describe how it felt as simply an empty feeling. The room which I shared with my sister Maria seemed empty. The dinner table which we shared as a family seemed empty. The house in which we lived seemed empty. The corner in the living room which Maria had claimed as her own seemed empty. Yes, empty. Our hearts and our minds were straining as we fought against that feeling of emptiness. Christmas was quickly approaching, and how I do not know, but there was a tree in the living room, all decorated and with presents lying beneath, presents for all of us, including Maria. And yet, it seemed empty. It was unnatural.

But the emptiness was not real; not real physically, mentally, or spiritually. Yes, Maria was lost, but never alone. We felt lost, but were never alone. Maria was taken sometime after 6:00 in the evening and by 8:00 our home and the streets of Sycamore were filled with people helping, searching, and consoling. People from all walks of life shared in our fears and anxiety. And this support never ended. This support has continued throughout the years. This support was and is there always because people were experiencing, at least to some extent, what we were experiencing; the horror of it all. Do you think it is by some strange coincidence that we were provided these efforts of all these people in the giving of support and comfort? I do not believe that is true for one minute. God knows what we need and when we need it. Today, as I look back, I can see Jesus standing there in our midst. I can see Jesus overseeing and directing. I don't remember seeing him then, but I see him so clearly now. And this is not just some image I have conjured up. I see him and I know with certainty that he is now and was then there among us!

God is our refuge and strength, an ever-present help in trouble.
Psalm 46:1

Prayer of thanksgiving for God's presence.

O Father of mercies, and God of all comfort, you have promised to be with me always. You have promised me refuge and strength. Father, I have seen your mighty hand. But I often do not sense your presence. I am often distracted. I often look elsewhere for strength and comfort. Forgive me Lord.

O Father of mercies, and God of all comfort, I thank you for all your goodness, including those that you surround me with as I feel empty and alone. Father, enable me to sense your presence, to recognize your help, and to grow in your strength. And this I pray in Jesus name. Amen.

As the days went by the search continued. For me it seemed as though time had stood still. But it didn't. The searches and the investigation came up empty. Maria was still missing. In the paper there was an announcement, "It is entirely possible that her dead body has been discarded in a field on a nearby farm…be alert for noticeable gatherings of crows and buzzards." I do not recall seeing this announcement at the time. Most likely my parents shielded me from the harshness of it, and rightly so. Even today the words sicken me. The night it appeared in the paper my sister Kay wrote in her diary, "Of all the nerve!" It is a thought, a possibility, which no loved one should ever have to experience.

Well, the events continue to unfold even today. It is Wednesday, March 30, 2016. It is 8:00 in the evening, and as I sit here writing these words I am at a loss as to what is going to happen over the next two days. Will Jack McCullough's conviction for the murder of my sister Maria be instantly overturned because of some misleading and incorrect information being put together by the current state's attorney? Or, will justice prevail? Today at 5:30 in the afternoon there was a knock on my door and I was informed of a hearing to be held in two days asking for a judge to release Jack McCullough. As I sit here waiting for some more information as to what this really means, I write these words to let you know that the events do continue to unfold. When you do not expect it, the unexpected often happens.

This new circumstance, this new twist in my life began to unfold on Good Friday, March 25, 2016. All of Lent, my home church of St. John, along with several of our sister congregations in the area, focused on the theme of *Broken*. And on Good Friday morning, just shortly before I was ready to leave to deliver a Good Friday message in worship, I received an email from the Dekalb County State's Attorney's office. The email informed me that they were requesting the reversal of the conviction of the person found guilty of the murder of my sister Maria. As I drove to neighboring Dekalb, to the place of worship, I too was broken. And I was broken not because of my sorrow and remorse over the crucifixion of my Lord and Savior Jesus Christ. No. I was broken over events and circumstances of the world. I had forgotten that Jesus said, *"In this world you will have trouble. But take heart! I have overcome the world."* I stopped and prayed. I prayed for forgiveness for the anger that I was feeling. I prayed for the Holy Spirit to enable me to rejoice in the certainty that the victory had been won by Christ Jesus at the cross... and more importantly at the empty tomb.

My sister Pat and I were beside ourselves. We felt abandoned by the system. We felt alone with no one to speak for us. It appeared that there was no one to challenge the misleading tactics of those now allied with Jack McCullough. On Good Friday evening my wife Diane and I attended worship at St. John Lutheran in Sycamore, Illinois. Pastor Weinhold's message was centered round the torn curtain, the Old Testament separation of the people from the presence of God. He talked about how Jesus died for our sins on the cross and the temple curtain was torn from top to bottom, signifying there was no longer any separation between us and God. As he spoke I was once again reminded to take heart! Jesus has overcome the world.

On Holy Saturday morning I received a phone call from retired Sycamore Police Chief Don Thomas. He began the conversation with these words, "I am calling to let you know that you are not alone." I interrupted saying, "But, we are alone!" He corrected me, and assured me that there were those who were at that very moment trying to figure out what can be done to get our voice heard. He said there was an effort being made to figure out how to get a special prosecutor appointed to oversee the case and that he would be in touch on Monday.

Almost immediately after I had finished talking with Chief Thomas I received a call from Julie Trevarthen. Julie was one of the assistant state's attorneys that had been instrumental in the successful prosecution at the original trial. She too was working on the idea of getting a special prosecutor appointed. She said that if I was willing, I had the right to file that motion in court under the Victim's Rights Act. I said that I would be willing to do whatever was necessary. She said she would get back to me with the details. And so, I waited.

Easter morning Diane and I went to church at St. John Lutheran in Sycamore. The Easter Victory Celebration was at hand. The theme of the celebration continued to follow the Lenten theme of *Broken*. Yes, the seal of the tomb had been broken! The victory had been won! The

Lord will reign forever! He will restore his broken people! We prayed, "Heavenly Father, today everything changes."

In this world you will have trouble. But take
heart! I have overcome the world.
John 16:33

Prayer: Lord let me trust in your victory.

O Lord, my God and Father in Christ Jesus, I praise you for who you are and the victory which has been won for me in Christ Jesus. But I must confess that sometimes I feel broken. Sometimes I wonder if justice will prevail. Sometimes I feel abandoned. Forgive me O Lord.

I thank you, O Lord, for in your great mercy you sent your only begotten Son to redeem me from sin, death, and the Devil. I thank you for the certainty that the victory has been won. I thank you for so clearly showing that you reign over all and that you will indeed restore your broken people. I thank you for your comforting words which insure us that we can take heart for Jesus has overcome the world.

O Lord, as the events in my life continue to unfold; as the unexpected often raises its head, may I know that I am not alone. May I sense your presence, and may I see those that you have placed in my life as instruments, as extensions of your almighty hand. Lord, enable me to rejoice and take heart in the victory which is mine in Christ Jesus, my Lord and my God. Amen.

Monday and Tuesday after Holy Week were like a blur as the events continued to unfold. Sunday night at about 9:00 Julie called saying that she would email me a sample of the format to be used for my motion for a special prosecutor to be appointed. As I began I realized that I had to do a better job of reviewing all of the state's attorney's assumptions. The entire process of preparing my motion lasted until 2:30 in the morning, after which I simply could not sleep. I could not sleep and I was to meet

Julie's father, also an attorney, at the courthouse at 8:30 in the morning so that he could walk me through the steps of filing the motion. I don't know how, but word of my motion spread like wildfire. The phone would simply not stop ringing. But the good news is that my motion was successful in that the judge, although he did not hear arguments on the motion, he did say that I was in fact entitled to have an attorney speak on our behalf. Yes. The events continue to unfold.

Last night, before I went to sleep, I thought: Maybe the Lord, through these newly unfolding events, was giving me the opportunity to share with you how I have grown, changed, and become stronger because of all of this.

I love you, O Lord, my strength. The Lord is
my rock, my fortress and my deliver.
Psalm 18:1-2

Prayer: I love you Lord. You are my strength.

Almighty God and Father, you have shown your power and your mighty hand over and over again. Almighty God and Father, I have seen my weakness. I know my frailties and failures. Yet I am often so slow in turning to my source of strength. Almighty God and Father, forgive me.

This journey has been long and hard. But Lord I thank you as you have led me over and over again to you and your strength. I love you Lord. You are my strength. I thank you, Almighty God and Father, that you have used this journey to help me grow; to help me change, and to help me become stronger. I pray now that you enable me by the power of the Holy Spirit to continue my turning to you, for you are my strength. In Jesus Christ my Lord, Amen.

On Sunday I will preach before my congregation that even in light of the fulfillment of the greatest promise ever accomplished on that first Easter morning, we forget. We forget the sweet promises of God. Oh, how life would be better if we only remembered. He says, *"I will never leave you or forsake you."* Yet when trouble comes, we feel all alone. He says, *"I will be with you always."* Yet there are times when we feel no one cares. He says, *"All things work together for good to those who love me."* Yet we cry out, "Why does this thing happen to me?" He says, *"My grace is sufficient for you."* Yet there are times when we feel that there is no help coming from anywhere. Yes life would be sweeter for us all, and we would not have to worry so much, if we only remembered that the One who conquered death is our daily companion.

This morning when I got up my wife Diane asked me how I was. I said, I am good. And, I am good. Yes, regardless of all the unfolding events, regardless of all the turmoil, I am good. The Lord is my strength. He has lifted me up. He has healed my brokenness.

Chapter Three

The Reliving

We all go through it: The what ifs? The if onlys. The maybes. The would of, could of, should ofs. We all go through it and oh how destructive they can sometimes be. And when they show their ugly head, the best advice you can hear, and I mean really hear, is simply just don't go there. Sounds easy doesn't it? But I think we all know that it is far from easy. No matter how certain you may be that there was simply nothing you could have done to change the outcome; no matter how far-fetched it is to think you had the power to change things, we all still ask the *what ifs*.

Jimmy McMillan lived on Archie Place just down the block from me in 1957. In fact he still lives in the same house today. He is four years younger than me, my sister Maria's age, seven years old at the time of Maria's kidnapping. Fifty-five years later, in September of 2012, while Jack McCullough was being tried for Maria's abduction and murder, he was plagued with that haunting question of "If only I had been there!"

Jimmy McMillan was walking home from school with some other kids including Kathy Sigman, who lived in the house down the lane just behind his, and Maria who lived just down the street. When you walked out of the front door of Jimmy's house and crossed Archie

Place, a street with so little traffic that we often played in it, you were on the playground of West Elementary School. That afternoon Maria and Kathy had gotten permission to play outside after supper. Kathy, on her way to Maria's had stopped at Jimmy's house to ask if he could also come out to play with them. His mother said no.

Standing on the steps of the DeKalb County Courthouse on the opening day of Jack McCullough's trial, Jimmy told reporters, "I was only seven years old but I have always thought that if my mother had let me go out that night I might have been able to do something to stop him." He was only seven years old. Even he admits he doesn't know what he could have done. And yet, now, for over fifty-five years he wonders "If only I had been there."

I have often been plagued with the *what ifs; the should of…the could ofs*, and how I deal with those times I will discuss later in the chapter on *Coping*. But I am thankful that I did not have to experience the feeling that I could have done something to change the outcome of this evil act. The feelings that my mother experienced as she asked herself "If only I had said no when she asked to go out and play." The feelings that my father experienced when he thought "If only I had been paying attention when she ran past me to get her doll!" The thoughts that Kathy might have had thinking, "If only I had gotten back sooner after going home to get my mittens." The thoughts that Chief Hindenburg might have had of thinking, "If only we had responded earlier." Yes. The *what ifs* can be a terrible thing.

Jimmy McMillan thought if he had been there it might have been different. We all like to think like Jimmy. We all like to think that we are difference makers. And sometimes we are. Yes. God often does use the little guy to make the huge difference in the world and in our lives. But we cannot undo what has been done. And we certainly cannot allow the *if only* kind of thinking to plague us. Yes, *allow* and *plague*. I chose those words carefully. You see it is you and I which allow that thinking to fill our minds, and those thoughts will without any doubt plague us; plague us even to the point of destruction.

Jesus said, "With man this is impossible,
but with God all things are possible."
Matthew 19:26

What if prayer.

O Almighty God, heavenly Father, you are indeed almighty, and I have seen your mighty deeds. Yet I am no different than others that think we are in control; that we can change things; that it is our fault when things go wrong. How foolish I am.

O Almighty God, you have told me and you have shown me that I cannot control all things. You have told me it is impossible. But all is not lost. You have said, "With God all things are possible." Now I pray, O Almighty God, that you relieve me of such foolish thoughts. I pray, O Almighty God, that you enable me to trust that after all is done, your might will prevail. Amen.

I go over it and over it in my mind. You've been there haven't you? It never really leaves you. For a time there is a reprieve, but then it comes back. It is different for each of us, but it is still there for us all. My sister Kay had everything played out in her mind. My sister Pat wanted and still wants every detail. I am different. I don't want to know the details of Maria's death. I just cannot bear the pain. But for all of us there are things we wish to know.

My sister Maria was kidnapped on December 3, 1957. It was not until the spring of 1958 that her little body was found. Months of waiting. Months of wondering. Where can she be? Is she alive? Who took her? How can this be? Yes. This period of time was really hard. There was really never any break in my thoughts. The void, except for the questions, was overwhelming. My mother begged for Maria's safe return saying that when she comes home there will be no more hand-me-downs for Maria; when she comes home they were really going to shop. My sister Kay prayed for Maria's return swearing to be a better

31

sister. My father, who seldom went to church with us, got down on his knees and prayed to God making a bargain that if he would just bring her back safe and sound, he would never again neglect his worship. My sister Pat and I seemed to keep our thoughts to ourselves.

On April 26, 1958, Mr. & Mrs. Frank Sitar from Hopkins, Minnesota, were hunting mushrooms while on a spring vacation in north-western Illinois. There in Jo Daviess County to their horror, they found not mushrooms, but the small body of a child. My sister Maria had been found. What happened to her? Who could have done such a thing? God, please help us! God, how could you have let this happen? "If only we had prayed harder", my sister Kay wrote in her diary, "Our minds were running out of control."

The pain which I felt, which we all felt, was unbearable. Our minds were filled with questions; questions which seemed to overpower us. It seemed as though that is all we could handle at the time was questions, unanswered questions. We had forgotten. We had allowed the unknown to overshadow the known. We were letting our minds wander away from the only absolute, the certainty that God loves us, and more importantly that God loves Maria.

> *For my thoughts are not your thoughts,*
> *neither are your ways my ways,*
> *declares the Lord.*
> *As the heavens are higher than the earth,*
> *so are my ways higher than your ways and*
> *my thoughts than your thoughts.*
> *Isaiah 55:8-9*

Prayer: Restore my thinking to center around Jesus.

Lord God Eternal, Healer of our souls, I have seen your great compassion as Jesus walked this earth healing with his words and the touch of his hand. I have seen the casting out of evil spirits, and I rejoice and praise you. But sometimes Lord, my pain is overwhelming. Sometimes Lord, my mind is filled with questions and fears. Oftentimes Lord, I too, like others, try bargaining with you. Lord, forgive me.

Lord God Eternal, I thank you for revealing your healing power. I thank you for showing me your great wisdom and your great love. Now, O Lord God, enable me to see beyond my limited vision; beyond my limited thought process. Enable me, O Lord God, to trust you. Enable me, O Lord God, to center my thinking round your great love as revealed so clearly in Jesus Christ, my Lord, and my Savior. Amen.

I was on a camping trip with the Boy Scouts on the weekend Maria was found, and the mother of one of my fellow scouts picked us up that Sunday. In the car she told me Maria had been found. I was numb and don't recall saying anything on the drive home. Immediately after arriving home my mother took me to my room. She said, "They found Maria." I asked, "Is she alive?" knowing that she was not. I never did tell my mother that someone had already told me. In fact, I never admitted that to anyone for another fifty-five years. I was twelve years old. I didn't cry. It must have been early when I arrived home that Sunday morning because we all, my father included, went to church. We sat in the back pew, which we never did. The sermon was directed toward us as well as the prayers. Our minds, my mind was swirling.

My sister, Maria Elizabeth Ridulph, was laid to rest on Wednesday, April 30, 1958. The Reverend Louis Going told those attending that they could find peace in knowing that Maria has reached her everlasting peace. He said, "We can be glad. We can have joy in the midst of this sorrow…if we know the gospel, if we know Christ." Reverend Going said, "She has found herself in the arms of her Lord and Savior." We were told that we could find peace.

Scene from the original funeral.

Leaving church at original funeral.

I did have peace knowing that Maria was in the arms of her Lord and Savior. But my life was forever changed. In the normal scheme of things Maria would have been known as my little sister, instead I became referred to as Maria's brother. My identity had changed. What happened on that dreadful December evening would always be a part of who I am. From that day on I would always be asked, "Are you related to that little girl who was kidnapped?"

Jesus said, "I have told you these things so
that in me you may have peace.
In this world you will have trouble.
But take heart! I have overcome the world."
John 16:33

Prayer for Peace

O God of peace and joy, I have seen my salvation as you have reconciled me to you in Christ Jesus my Lord. You have brought peace to the world. You have brought peace between me and you my Creator. But I must confess that I often do not recognize the peace and joy which are mine. My mind swirls and grows numb.

O God of peace and joy, I thank you for the certainty by which I know that Maria now has the ultimate peace and joy as she rests in the arms of Jesus. I pray that you give me this peace also. I know that this peace and joy are mine to have right now. Enable me to lay hold of them. In Jesus Name. Amen.

Time went on, but Maria was never far from our thoughts. Then, on June 30, 2011, the reliving of this evil event in our lives was going to shift into high gear. I had spent the day in Bloomington, Illinois, at a funeral. My brother-in-law Bill, my sister Pat's husband, had just lost his brother along with his wife in a terrible automobile accident. It was a sad day. Of all the funerals I had been at, many of which I had officiated, I had never been to a double funeral. So sad to see two coffins being carried up to the front of the church.

It was 6:00 in the evening when I pulled into my driveway returning from Bloomington, and I wasn't even out of the car when my wife Diane came running out of the house to greet me. She had not gone to the funeral since it was a week day and she was watching our grandson Keegan. As I opened the car door she blurted out that they had found the guy who killed my sister Maria. She said I had to call the states attorney right away. Of course I asked when he had called and what else he had to say, but Diane didn't know anything else; just that I had to call him.

When I got into the house I called State's Attorney Clay Campbell and he asked if he and a Sycamore police detective could come right over to talk to me about my sister's case. Within ten minutes they were at the door. He introduced himself since we had never officially met, and he introduced me to Detective Dan Hoffman whom I knew from my contact with him as a chaplain with the Sycamore Police Department. He didn't waste any time. He said we know who killed your sister Maria: Jack McCullough. I didn't recognize the name, but then he said I would have known him as John Tessier. I gasped. Someone I knew had killed Maria.

They didn't go into any great detail but said that there was no doubt that he had killed Maria, but proving it might be another matter. They told me that the video of his interrogation was being downloaded as we spoke and that would be the deciding factor as to whether or not they would issue a warrant for his arrest. He asked if I would like him to call me when he made the decision. I said yes.

At approximately 10:00 that night I received the call from Clay Campbell. They were issuing a warrant for his arrest along with a request for his extradition back to Illinois to stand trial. He warned me that the press would be all over this and offered to shield us from them as much as they possibly could. He even offered to put up a road block on our street. I couldn't imagine that would be necessary. After all, this was a 54 year old case. How wrong I turned out to be. I called my sisters

Pat and Kay to tell them what was happening. The ordeal had begun. The next day when the news broke the calls were non-stop. And when we stopped answering calls the press was soon knocking at our door. And when we tried to leave the house they blocked the driveway. When I did get out of the driveway they stopped me in the street. I just could not believe it.

It wasn't until after the trial that I found out that the judge did not want to issue the arrest warrant. Clay Campbell had to call upon Sycamore Police Chief Don Thomas to help persuade the judge that this was the right thing to do. They were arresting someone I had known for killing my sister. On July 2, 2011, I wrote in my journal, "My emotions are running high and it is hard to think of anything else; even in my dreams."

O Lord…you are familiar with all my ways.
How precious to me are your thoughts, O God!
Search me, O God, and know my heart;
Test me and know my anxious thoughts.
Psalm 139

Prayer: God know my heart. Change my thought.

Lord God, Loving Father, you see and know all things, especially you see and know me, and I am thankful for that since I often do not know myself. I pray, Lord God, search me and know my heart. Test me and know my anxious thoughts. The ordeal has begun, and my emotions are high, and it is hard to think of anything else. You, O Lord, are familiar with all my ways; put me at ease. I pray this in confidence, in Jesus name. Amen.

Once you have put a face, a name, to the cause of the evil, everything changes. For us, for me, once I knew who had killed my sister, everything changed. It changed for the worse. Now that I knew the person, a neighbor, the questions in my mind were endless. Now it seemed as though all my thoughts were on my sister Maria and to what happened to her so very long ago. And it was long ago; fifty-four years ago. But to me it was happening right now; in the present. Several people have commented that it is too bad my parents were not alive to see this day. But they just don't understand. It is horrible reliving such a thing. In fact it is worse than reliving. Something new is unfolding nearly every day it seems. Things I just don't want to know, and yet I just can't stop thinking about. I am so thankful that my parents were not alive to go through this. I am so thankful that my parents are with Maria, far above and beyond all this, in heaven, in the arms of our Lord and Savior. But we are here. Pat, Kay, and I are here. And it is a terrible time!

On July 26, 2011, I wrote in my journal: "I don't know where to start…so much has happened and continues to happen. We all went on vacation for ten days and it was good to get away, but even that was hectic. This week I preached on Isaiah 55:1 where the Lord tells us to come and buy without money, without cost. WOW! God's love is our possession; always, especially when we need it most. I am thankful that I have been able to help Pat and Kay through this difficult time. Tomorrow they extradite Tessier and they exhume Maria's body. How hard this is. Diane (my wife) has been a great comfort!"

> *As a mother comforts her child, so will I comfort you.*
> *Isaiah 66:13*

Prayer for God's comfort.

O God of Comfort and God of Love, I know of your splendor. I know of your promise to comfort me. But here I am and it is a horrible time. Things have changed for the worse and I can't stop thinking about it. It is so painful reliving such a thing. But I also know of your mercies. I am so thankful that Maria and my parents are far above and beyond all this, in heaven, in the arms of our Lord and Savior. I pray that you enable me to concentrate on the fact that your love, O Lord, is my possession now, and always, especially when I need it the most. Yes, Lord, help me to not only know of your great love and comfort, but to rely upon it. Amen.

You know, sometimes we can feel overwhelmed. Sometimes we can feel so lost or alone. But that is never true. God is always with us. And God will give us what we need to sustain us in the most difficult of circumstances. And I thank God for the comfort and support of my family and loved ones!

God is our refuge and strength, an ever-present help in trouble.
Therefore we will not fear, though the earth give way and the mountains
fall into the heart of the sea, though its waters roar and foam and
the mountains quake with their surging.
Psalm 46:1-3

You are my hiding place;
you will protect me from trouble and surround
me with songs of deliverance.
Psalm 32:7

Prayer in thanksgiving for support of family and friends.

Dear Father in Heaven, you have called me to be your child. You have adopted me into your glorious family, and I rejoice in that. You have also placed me into my loving family here on earth, and blessed me with a host of friends, and I rejoice in that as well. I pray, Dear Father, that as you give us strength, and surround us with songs of deliverance, that you enable each of us here on earth to strengthen and help one another. Amen.

My sister Kay thrived on working things out in her mind, and when her mind was made up that was it. She had figured it out, and that was it. Well, the more information we received about Johnny Tessier (now known as Jack McCullough) the more she had to work with. She had come to the conclusion that he could not have acted alone, therefore, it simply made sense to her that his father Ralph had to have helped him. With the information we had been provided there was no doubt in our minds that Jack McCullough, whom we had known from the neighborhood, had killed our sister Maria. On the other hand, I told Kay that I could not believe that Ralph had known anything about it. You see, I had gotten to know Ralph Tessier from Alcoholics Anonymous. He and I had attended AA meetings together and I just could not believe that he could have lived with such a secret for all these years.

At the time Maria was kidnapped, I knew who the Tessiers were. I knew what Ralph and John looked like, but did not know much else about them. But later in life I did get to know Ralph, not only through AA, but also I used his services as a sign painter. He was a sign painter, actually quit gifted, and I had him make several signs to be used at the tavern I owned. On several occasions I was even in his home, the same home in which the Tessiers lived in 1957. He was very active in AA, and from hearing him speak on many occasions I just could not believe that he knew anything about my sister's murder. I could just not bring myself to believe this person, who I knew in his sobriety, could have lived with the knowledge of such a terrible evil act. At the rape trial of Jack McCullough's sister, I asked one of Jack's sisters directly if her father could have been involved in any way. The other siblings were present, however, I was never given an answer to indicate one way or another.

And yet, here we were, both Kay and I playing this over in our minds trying to figure it out, while my sister Pat simply wanted all the details of my sister's death to be finally revealed. My sister Kay died of cancer on September 26, 2011, joining her husband Larry, my mother and father, along with little Maria, never knowing if her theory was correct. Pat and I remained behind to suffer through what was yet to come.

Jesus said, *"You will know the truth, and the truth will set you free."* *John 8:31-32.* You know, we all want to know the truth. We all have the desire to figure things out, and some, like my sister Kay, think that they can. Others are plagued with the process throughout their entire lives. Our minds just don't want to let it go. Some of us just need to know everything. My sister Kay, my father, and my mother, never heard the truth as laid out in court. Instead they received something better by far. They joined Maria in the arms of Truth, Christ Jesus our Lord. Pat and I on the other hand remain behind, and try, with the help of God, to stay focused on what is really important.

> *But what does it matter?*
> *The important thing is that in every way,*
> *whether from false motives or true,*
> *Christ is preached. And because of this I rejoice.*
> *Philippians 1:18*

Prayer on truth/importance

God of Mercy and of Truth, I come before you today seeking the real Truth, which is Jesus Christ himself. So often I look for worldly truth to serve as my master. So often I seek answers to my questions as though the answers will alleviate my pain, my frustration, my worry, and my anguish.

I thank you, O God of Mercy and of Truth, for showing me the path. Jesus said, "I am the Way, the Truth, and the Light." Enable me, O Lord, to see that the important thing is that in every way I see Christ Crucified. Enable me to rejoice in the truth that heaven is the goal. Enable me to listen to you O God of Mercy and Truth, and let me rejoice. Amen.

Pat, my brother-in-law Bill, and I met with State's Attorney Clay Campbell and the prosecution team after the rape trial on Monday, April 23, 2012. We met at 2:30 PM in the conference room of the state's attorney's office. Pat recalls it as a relaxed atmosphere, and I suppose it was because by this time we had gotten to know them fairly well.

We began by discussing the rape case. I was very direct in expressing my opinion that it appeared that the witnesses had not been properly prepped for their testimony. We had questions as to why the past sexual abuse that had taken place in the home, as well as the neighborhood, was not presented. We also discussed the fact that it was not a good idea to have publicly criticized the judge. Clay had just spoken out of frustration. I understood his frustration; I think we all did.

When Jack McCullough was pronounced innocent cries of anguish were heard throughout the courtroom. His sister Kathy cried out, "Why didn't she let me testify!" His entire family cried as they held one another. Bob Tessier, Jack McCullough's brother said, "This is a travesty of justice." Jeanne Tessier and Michelle Weinman's boyfriend both said, "The system sucks!" But I was not overly surprised because it really boiled down to "He says – She says". Even the judge's comments pointing out flaws in the prosecutor's case did not at the time upset me. My first thought was that she lashed out because she knew he was guilty and was disturbed to have to rule otherwise. But later I found out that was not the case.

The judge publically accused Clay Campbell of not asking pertinent questions which may have influenced her decision. Questions, which I later learned she had ruled in the pre-trial motions, that were not allowed. I also was told by two different court employees that it was normally her practice of asking that type of question herself during this type of trial. My question now was why didn't she ask those questions if she felt they were important? Clay Campbell had told us that the judge was a good person; fair and impartial. My sister Pat now told him, "I just don't see it. Her actions do not reflect it." We were now concerned. I was angry. I was irate!

A fool gives full vent to his anger,
But a wise man keeps himself under control.
Proverbs 29:11

Prayer on anger.

Almighty God, Author of life and health, you see my anguish. You see my frustration and my concern. You see my anger. I ask you now to forgive me. I ask you now to aid me in moving beyond such feelings that can only distract and hurt.

I thank you Almighty God, because you have so clearly shown that you are indeed the Author of life and health. I thank you Almighty God, that you have shown so clearly that for my own good, you can, as you have in the past, lift me up and relieve me of these harmful feelings.

I pray now for that deliverance. I pray now that you would move me beyond these things which can injure and blind. And I pray this in confidence for you are the Author of life and health. Amen.

Our conversation turned to Maria's case, and with it the question that was on all of our minds, did we stand a chance with the presiding judge? We left the meeting frustrated and concerned. However, we did feel that the team had learned a great deal from the rape case as to how to proceed. They assured us that there would be no chance that Kathy Chapman would not be properly prepped for testimony. At this point it appeared that the case really rested on her identification.

On August 3, 2012, Judge Stuckert stepped down on her own from presiding over the murder trial. My wife Diane and I were vacationing with the kids and grandkids, including my daughter Maria and her family, in Kentucky and then Tennessee, so we did not hear this news until our return ten days later. This news came as a surprise and with a great sigh of relief. Now we did not have to go through the difficult, almost impossible task of trying to have her removed from the case.

The Dekalb County Chronicle wrote, "We doubt that a veteran judge such as Stuckert would let personal feelings about the state's attorney cloud her judgment, especially in such an important case. However, her decision to remove herself was wise. No matter how Stuckert eventually ruled in McCullough's murder trial, either side could claim she was influenced by previous events." As to why it appeared that Stuckert had it in for Campbell I have never been able to find out, but this I know, there was so much political tension in that court house you could not cut it with a blow torch. I never would have believed it if I had not seen it. At one time they worked together at the same law firm; perhaps it started there, but it must have gone deeper than that. I just don't know, and I have asked several people.

The pre-trial motions began on August 21, 2012, with Judge James Hallock presiding. He had been brought over from neighboring Kane County to replace Judge Stuckert. My sister Pat and her husband Bill made the trip to join me in attending every hearing. They had to drive from either Morris or El Paso Illinois, a distance of one to two hours each way, since they were in the process of moving at the time. Now the process had become intent. Not only were we reliving past events, but we were listening to details concerning evidence. Each pre-trial hearing brought with it something new, something new to add to our already cluttered minds. If this happened, this could not have happened. If this didn't happen, this might have happened. This might have happened, but you can't suggest that it did. This did happen, but you can't say that it did. My mind was working a mile a minute.

In my journal the thought for the day was taken from 1 Peter 5:9-10. It read, "Keep a firm grip on the faith…It won't be long before this generous God who has great plans for us in Christ…will have you put together and on your feet for good." I wrote, "The pre-trial motions for Maria's case began with a new judge. I know this was by the hand of God. 'Keep a firm grip on the faith'…Pat & I are growing closer as we support one another. Diane has been great!"

You know, during times of great stress, especially during times of reliving great tragedies, times filled with painful memories, and times of some confusion, we can lose focus can't we? But as difficult as this time was, Pat and I talked about how we might possibly see the good which might come out of it all.

And we know that in all things God works
for the good of those who love him.
Romans 8:28

Prayer on seeing the good in every circumstance.

Blessed Father in heaven, you have shown your goodness, your power, and your love, over and over again. You have told me of your great plans for me. Yet I become concerned and frustrated. My mind becomes cluttered. My mind often works against all that you want for me. But in the midst of all this turmoil, I praise you, and I thank you, as I see so clearly your hand, your presence, putting things in their rightful place, showing your influence in all things, just as you promised.

Blessed Father in heaven, I pray that by the power of the Holy Spirit you would keep me in the faith. I pray that you enable me to experience that great sigh of relief. I pray that you would put me on my feet for good, as I search, and as I see, the good things which you have promised. Amen.

Several years ago, in the early 1990's, a woman, along with another woman who I believe was her daughter, came to our tavern one Sunday afternoon specifically to talk with me about my sister Maria. My daughter Diane was working at the time, and called me to come out and speak with them. This woman gave me a convincing story indicating that her husband had killed Maria, and she was compelled to tell me since the police officials refused to listen to her. I really believed there might be something to the story.

At that time I had built a relationship with one of our customers, Gordon Plunket, who was a detective with the Dekalb County Police Department, and I called him to ask what I should do with this information. Several days later he put me in touch with Pat Solar of the Sycamore Police Department, and we arranged to meet. Detective Solar informed me that he had been working on this case, on his own time, for several years. It was as he said a passion for him. He assured me that when this information had been previously brought to their attention, the husband was ruled out since at the time he was in the Army stationed in Germany.

Several years later, Pat Solar called me at home asking to meet with me and my family indicating that he had news regarding who had killed Maria. This call did not come as a complete surprise since I was aware that he had been working on this case for several years, and yet it certainly peaked my interest to say the least. After the phone call I called my sisters Pat and Kay, along with my father and mother and made an appointment to meet with Solar. I don't recall that any of us had any high expectations at the time.

We met with Pat Solar at the Sycamore Police Department in what served as an officer break room, conference room, and I believe was also called a "situation room". Introductions were made, beverages were offered, and Solar began to present his case. He began to tell us about a convicted child killer who had died in prison who had bragged to another inmate about killing another little girl. He was convinced that this second little girl was Maria.

During the meeting he said that he had boxes of files which he had accumulated over the years on Maria's case. He started to read about blood on Maria's neck and I stopped him. My sister Kay and I did not want to know about it. My sister Pat did want to know as much as possible about Maria's death and it was here that Solar gave her a copy of the autopsy report. Later Pat said that on her first attempt to read the report she couldn't do it. It was just too hard. Later she said that she was able to read the entire report by starting at the back and reading toward the front. To this day I have not read the report. In fact, many years later, when we were asked to participate in a special Dr. Phil Show featuring our case, I asked them not to talk about the autopsy report which they seemed so interested in doing. I am so thankful that they were sympathetic in honoring my request.

After his presentation Solar asked what we thought. My father spoke up saying, "What difference does it make?" My sister Pat had concerns from the beginning that his name was not John or Johnny. We all had concerns since his age didn't match the description given by Kathy. He would have been much older at the time of the kidnapping. Solar explained it away saying first of all that the killer most likely would not have used his real name. This made sense. Concerning his age Solar said that an eight year old's recognition of age could not be depended upon. This to me did not make sense, except I did realize that to a young child anyone who was older and taller would be considered as old. We were not convinced but did not object to his closing his investigation.

On November 5, 1997, the headline of the *Sycamore News* read, "The Ridulph Murder Case is Closed." Case closed; except the very next day after one news article proclaimed the case was solved, another paper showed convincing evidence that this could not have been the killer. We were not surprised. There were claims that Solar had self-serving motives for breaking the story as he had recently applied for the position of Police Chief of Sycamore. I do not believe that was the case. I believe he was sincere but had overlooked obvious flaws in his investigation.

My father said, "What difference does it make?" The Bible tells us, "We know that in all things God works for the good of those who love him." Well, what difference does it make? And how can we possibly find any good in such evil?

Well, I never really gave much consideration to these two questions until near the end of the trial of Jack McCullough for the murder of my sister Maria. And, in the overall picture, in the final end of things as we know them, these questions really do not matter. But, for today, they do. I have come to see that it matters to the thousands of people who are searching for answers, for justice, in cases of unsolved crimes, especially crimes of missing or murdered loved ones. I see the good which God has promised me. In part it has been revealed in the healing which I have experienced during this painful process. I see the good which is coming to me as I write these words, and I anticipate that God will use these words of mine to bring healing to others as well.

Jack McCullough (John Tessier) was arrested on July 29, 2011, for the kidnapping and murder of my sister Maria Ridulph in Seattle, Washington. During the preparation for his trial, the state's attorney's office discovered that he had also raped his sister. As the details of that crime unfolded, it was decided that he could and should also be charged and tried for that crime. Now the question was which case should be tried first. My sister and I feared that he would be tried first for the rape and found guilty, and because he would be going to prison for that crime he would not be tried on the more difficult fifty-five year old case of Maria's murder.

When the decision was made to prosecute McCullough on the rape case first, State's Attorney Clay Campbell came to my home to inform us prior to releasing the news to the press. When he heard of our concerns about the possibility of not proceeding with the murder case he assured us that would not happen. What difference did it make? I am not sure I can answer that question. But this I know: It made a difference! As hard as we knew a trial was going to be on us, there was no question in our minds that it had to be done. We did not want him convicted for some other crime. We did not want a plea bargain. We wanted him tried for what he did to our sister. Today as I think about this, the only thing I know for sure is that had he not been prosecuted for this evil deed, we would have been left with a sort of emptiness. My sister Pat wanted what he had done to be fully revealed. At the time I don't know what I wanted. But today as I look back I see that I needed what was to come. I needed to cry. I needed to heal.

There is a time for everything...a time to search and a time to give up...
A time to tear and a time to mend...a time to love and a time to hate...
Ecclesiastes 3:1-8

Prayer on crying and healing

Gracious Father in heaven, you have told me to be still and know that you are God. You have told me there is a time to search and a time to give up. You have told me there is a time to tear and a time to mend. Yet it is hard. I am often confused. Sometimes there are things which I long to know, and then there are things which are just too hard to bring to mind. Sometimes I just don't want to hear it. But, Gracious Father in heaven, today I thank you for the assurance that you are always with me in all circumstances. I thank you Father that you have enabled me to see a glimpse of the good that you have promised me.

Gracious Father in heaven, you have given me a time to tear and a time to mend. And I pray that you continue revealing to me the good. I pray that you continue to let me cry. I pray that you continue to let me heal. In Jesus Name. Amen.

The rape trial had begun and I wrote in my journal: "The rape trial started for Jack McCullough (John Tessier). My sister Pat wanted to go, and at first I went simply in support of her, but I am glad that I did go. It sure gave me a different view of the court system. As I was thinking about who else could testify as to some of the events back then, I realized how many of those guys were dead because of alcohol abuse. I thank God since I could have been one of them!"

Later in my journal I wrote: "McCullough was found not guilty of the rape of his sister. The judge really handcuffed the prosecution and then publically criticized them…so much politics. The pre-trial motions for Maria's case began with a new judge. I know this was by the hand of God. *Keep a firm grip on the faith.* Pat and I are growing closer as we support one another. Diane has been great! The theme for the day in my journal was: *To keep a firm grip on the faith…It won't be long before this generous God who has great plans for us in Christ…will have you put together and on your feet for good."*

On September 8, 2012, the theme for the day in my journal was, *I trusted him when the roses were blooming, I trust him now.* I wrote,

"Maria's trial starts next week and I am scheduled to be interviewed by "48 Hours" on Sunday. I don't really know how I feel about that. We take everything for granted when the roses are blooming, but I am so glad that I can trust in the Lord when they are not!"

The rape trial began at the DeKalb County Court House with the press out in force. I don't know for sure, but I believe that State's Attorney Clay Campbell had made it clear to them that we should be left alone, and for the most part we were. There was this one guy, Peter Henderson from CBS News/48 Hours here from New York, who quietly introduced himself to us. He said that at some point in time he would like to talk to us if we were willing. Nothing else was said. During the trial I learned that CBS had already committed to featuring our case on the 48 Hours program, and had even begun filming some interviews and locations at the court house. It was the kindness that Peter Henderson showed us from the very beginning that led us to agree in participating in the show.

On Saturday, September 8, 2012, three days before the trial of Jack McCullough for the murder of my sister Maria was to begin, I spent the morning with Assistant State's Attorney Victor Escarcida. I was to be the first witness in the trial. Victor explained that I was being called simply to give some background information about our family, our home, and the community at large. He would then ask me to give my recollection of the events which occurred on the night in which Maria was abducted. He explained the layout of the courtroom, and most of all assured me that I would not be prohibited from watching the remainder of the trial. He said that my testimony was of a nature that there would be no need to recall me at a later time for further testimony. I made it clear that if that was not the case then I would not be able to testify. We then went over the questions to be asked and my responses.

On Sunday, September 9, 2012, the day before the trial, I was interviewed for the documentary 48 Hours was planning on airing on CBS Television. That evening I wrote in my journal, "The people from 48 Hours interviewed me today. They were great, especially Emily Wichick. She was so young and treated me as though she knew me forever. (Over time I would come to love her!) The interview process was easy but I became emotional at points."

Going back in my mind, actually reliving the events of that horrible night, was very difficult. It was kind of like watching a movie, except the events were real. It was kind of like having a bad dream, except you didn't wake-up and the memory of it was gone. In fact it was much worse. I was forcing myself to remember things long forgotten. Things which I did not want to remember. Things which were so painful. It is hard to explain really. Maybe the best way to describe it is that it is like this dark cloud coming over you; a dark cloud which threatens to consume you. I think that those of you that have experienced this will know what I am saying.

My interview with Erin Moriarty of "48 Hours" took place at the Northern Illinois University campus in neighboring Dekalb, Illinois, about eight miles from my home. I was instructed to wear something dark for the camera, and Emily Wichick picked me up at my home. On the drive I directed her past the house where the Tessier family had lived on Center Cross Street. We then proceeded to the corner of Center Cross and Archie Place where Maria was last seen, which was only five houses away. We turned onto Archie Place and drove past my childhood home, and then down the block to the home where Kathy Sigman had lived. As I pointed out these places Emily would stop the car to take it all in. When we arrived at the university location for the filming of the interview, Emily introduced me to Erin and the camera and sound staff. They all made me feel at ease.

The interview began with a simple request; Erin asked me to tell her about Maria. I don't know why, but this caught me totally off guard. I broke down. After a brief pause, we continued with the interview.

The next day the trial began, and after opening statements, I was called as the first witness. After telling the court who I was, where I was from, and a description of our home back in 1957, along with a description of the community, I was asked to tell the court about Maria. I again broke down.

That which should come natural; simply sharing with others what a wonderful little girl my sister was, became almost impossible to tell.

By the rivers of Babylon we sat and wept.
Psalm 137

Prayer on weeping over what is lost.

Dear Father in heaven, you know, see, and rule over all things. And it is in this I find strength. Father, I have been forced to go back over things in my mind, to remember things long forgotten, things I did not want to remember. Father, it seems as though a dark cloud threatens to consume me, and I was caught off guard, I broke down.

But, dear Father in heaven, I am thankful that I can trust in you at all times, especially at times when things seem so dark. I pray now that you enable me to see beyond the darkness. I pray now that you enable me to joyfully share with others what a wonderful little girl Maria was. I pray that you remove that dark cloud which threatens to consume me. I pray that you allow me to see only the brightness and the glory of your love as Jesus holds Maria in his loving arms. Amen.

Before the trial for my sister's murder began, in fact on the same day in which Jack McCullough was being transported back to Sycamore from Seattle Washington in order to stand trial, Maria's body was exhumed from her earthly resting place. This is one of the hardest things I have ever in my life experienced. Several days before this took place, State's Attorney Clay Campbell phoned me at my home and asked if he might come over. When he arrived he came right to the point; they wanted my permission to exhume Maria's body. I gasped, "Oh no!" And I cried. I was shocked! I should have expected it. Many had told me that was more than a possibility. But I was caught totally off guard. Even though I sensed that my permission really was not necessary, I said yes. I told them you need to do what needs to be done.

Among my people are wicked men...Their evil deeds have no limit...
A horrible and shocking thing has happened.
Jeremiah 5:26-30

Prayer on horrible and shocking things.

Lord God, Creator of all things, you are my everything, and I rejoice in the knowledge that you are there for me at all times and in all circumstances. Lord God, I have come face to face with one of the hardest things I have ever had to experience, and my response was tears and shock. Lord God, you have told me that I would be tested in this world, and I have been. You have told me that before Jesus comes again in all his glory to judge, I will face even more hard times and trials. I have cried, and I have been shocked. But I thank you Lord God, for you were there to lift me up.

Lord God, Creator of all things, I live among wicked people and in wicked times. I pray, O Lord, for your continued protection. You, O Lord, the Creator of all things, are in control of all things. Therefore, I pray that you take control of me O Lord; of me and my emotions. I pray that I may live in peace rather than the turmoil and shock which surrounds me. I pray all this in confidence. In you, Lord God, Creator of all things visible and invisible. Amen.

Maria's body had been taken to the University of Indiana for analysis. During the trial I was told by the prosecution team that at some point an expert would be called to testify in detail as to the cause of her death. They told me that when that time came I would be given an opportunity to leave the court room. This would be a graphic explanation accompanied with video. When the time came I left the court room. My sister Pat chose to remain. I had spared myself for the moment from that which I chose not to see or hear. However, shortly later, the horrible became even worse. My sister Pat and I were seated in the front row of seats directly behind the table provided for the prosecution team. I don't recall at what point the trial was in, but the assistant state's attorney rose from the table, and as he did he picked up an 8X10 photograph of my sister's badly decomposed body. Unknowingly, the photo was exposed directly in front of me. I can hardly write these words. This image of my beloved little Maria is forever etched in my mind. *Among my people are wicked men...Their evil deeds have no limit...A horrible and shocking thing has happened.*

That horrible image has been implanted into my mind even though from the very beginning, that day in that court room, I have tried to block it out. It comes to me unexpected and uninvited like a flashback. And, just as quickly as it tries to show itself, I cast it out.

Last Sunday, January 31, 2016, I preached on two miracles which Jesus performed (Luke 4:31-34). Both miracles had to do with healing. The first was when Jesus was confronted by a man possessed by a demon, an evil or unclean spirit, and Jesus responds sternly: "Be quiet! Come out of him!" And the demon left him. The second miracle involved the healing of Simon's mother-in-law who was suffering from a high fever. Jesus bent over her, rebuked the fever, and it left her. I went on to talk about how Jesus stands over us in our feverish condition as well. When Simon's mother-in-law opened her eyes and looked up she saw the Lord Jesus standing over her, and we may do the same. He will touch us and rebuke the fever. Just as the winds and the waves heard his rebuke, and from their roar they hushed themselves to a great calm, so will he see our difficulties, hear our pleas, stand over us, touch us, lift us up, rebuke our fever, and restore our joy.

That horrible photo of my sister is a fever, an evil, which must be cast out. It is an evil which would consume me more than any physical fever you can imagine. But, when it flashes itself, I thank God that he takes it from me, he rebukes it, and replaces it with the precious memory of my innocent little Maria.

Deliver me according to your promise.
Psalm 119:170

Prayer on deliverance

Gracious God, Heavenly Father, I have seen your marvelous light in Christ Jesus my Lord. I know of your mighty deeds. I know of your fulfillment of promises, as not one word has failed of all the good promises you gave! And yet I have also seen the horrible become even worse. But praise be to you, Gracious God, my Heavenly Father, for I have seen you cast it out.

Father, I have seen Jesus as he stands over me in my feverish condition, and I have felt his touch. And I thank you!

I pray now that you instill within me the sure knowledge that you will continue to see my difficulties, hear my pleas, stand over me, touch me, lift me up, rebuke my fever, and restore my joy. In Jesus Name. Amen.

Jack McCullough's trial for the murder of my sister Maria lasted for one week. A trying week to be sure. But one in which we were surrounded by love...love of family, love of friends, neighbors, and even strangers. But most of all the love of God manifested in so many ways. I just don't know what I would have done as I relived, as I lived through this horrible tragedy in my life, without the influence and the presence of God. You see, recognizing and dealing with evil can be very dangerous! It can take you to the darkest of places, and left to your own you may never come out. I have to ask, because I just cannot understand, how can anyone go through these trials without knowing, no, more than just knowing, but without trusting in God?

I am not going to share with you the details of the trial. I am not going to share with you the details of my walking through the events of those dreadful days in December of 1957. But this I will say, I thank God for putting so many supportive people in my life. You see, then, and even now, the love and support so graciously given overpowered the dark thoughts that were invading and trying to overtake me. It is hard to explain, but the evil which could have taken over, and I mean taken over not only then, but taken over permanently, was not only diminished but defeated by the love so richly outpoured. The evil, as powerful as it is, became less. The evil has become a bad memory instead of a driving force. We pray in the Lord's Prayer *deliver us from evil,* and our prayer is answered, *for thine is the kingdom and the power and the glory forever and ever. Amen.*

> *Because of the Lord's great love we are not*
> *consumed, for his compassions never fail.*
> *Lamentations 3:22*

Prayer on love prevails.

Our Father which art in heaven, you have beckoned me to come to you in prayer. And I come to you and ask that you deliver me from evil. Dark thoughts have been invading and trying to overtake me. Father, I know that dealing with evil can be very dangerous. I know that dealing with evil can take me to the darkest of places, places from which I may never return. But I praise you Father, for you heard my cries. I praise you Father, for you surround me with love, the love of family, friends, neighbors, and even strangers. But most of all Father, you surround me with your love which you manifest in so many ways.

I thank you Father, for I would be lost without your presence and your influence. I thank you for putting so many supportive people in my life. Yes, Father, the evil is diminished by the love. The evil is defeated and becomes but a bad memory instead of a driving force. Yes, I thank you Father for your love. Amen.

Chapter Four

The Coping

Maria was kidnapped in December of 1957. I was eleven years old. In the fall of 1958 I began weekly instruction for the rite of confirmation of my faith, and on April 10, 1960 I was confirmed. I was fourteen. It was at that time that Pastor Carl Kruse planted the seed that I might want to consider studying for the ministry. In the fall of 1960, three years after Maria was kidnapped, I left for Concordia College in Milwaukee, Wisconsin to enter prep-school for the ministry.

I have been asked many times if the tragic loss of my sister had influenced my decision to study for the ministry. I can only say this: I don't know. But this I do know: The kidnapping and murder of Maria, without any doubt, changed and influenced who I was from the very moment she was taken from us.

Maria was kidnapped when I was eleven. By the time I was thirteen I was drinking at every opportunity, sometimes even going back to school after drinking some wine during lunch time. By the time I was fourteen I was drinking on a regular basis. By the time I was sixteen I was drinking on a daily basis. I have been asked if Maria's tragic death led me to alcohol. Many times people have commented that it is no wonder that I drank because of the pain which this brought into our lives. But to that question I can truthfully say that I had a tendency to like the taste of wine and its affect even before Maria was gone. Did this event influence my pre-existing problem with alcohol? Here again I can only say that Maria's murder influenced my very being.

During my junior year at Concordia College (Prep-school) my drinking was out of control. All I did was drink. I was kicked off the basketball team for drinking, which was a major blow to me. It still bothers me to this day. My grades took a nose dive. My parents were in the process of getting a divorce. And I was asked not to return. Here again, it was a different time then, and alcohol was not really considered to be the addiction that it is today. Therefore, my drinking was not seen as anything more than unacceptable behavior. I was seventeen.

I enrolled for my senior year of high school at the Sycamore Community High School. I continued to drink daily; often times intoxicated by mid-day at school. I already had enough credits to graduate from high school so my study habits didn't really matter. My journey to the ministry was on hold to say the least.

In September of 1963, I met a girl at a party who was new to Sycamore. There was a lot of drinking going on which was usual for my senior class, and Betty and I really hit it off. Our first official date was at her brother's wedding. There was a lot of drinking at the reception, and after we left, I was drunk. Get this: I took her to the cemetery to see Maria's grave. It was dark, and in my drunken state I couldn't find the grave. What a first date. In December we were secretly married with the aid of a Kane County clerk. To say the least she was not using very good judgment. Betty was sixteen. I was seventeen. It was six years after I was considered a child; six years after Maria's murder.

In 1963, I was an alcoholic, a teen aged husband, secretly married, no longer studying for the ministry, and my parents were in the process of getting a divorce. In 1964 I graduated from high school and was off to Chicago to study engineering. Why I don't know, except I was looking for what I thought would be an easy career, even though I was certainly not gifted in that area. For the time being my wife went to Michigan to stay with her mother. The school I was going to, Allied Institute of Technology, placed me into my first real job just weeks after school started. My mother was paying for school and also for my rent at the YMCA Hotel on Wabash Ave in Chicago. All the money I had was the money I had received as gifts from graduation from high school.

Here I am, now eighteen years old in Chicago, supposed to be going to school, living at the YMCA, working at Ryerson Steel on the south side in the warehouse, and broke with my first paycheck not coming for two weeks.

I met this guy staying at the YMCA Hotel on Wabash Avenue. He was black, and he was gay. I think at first he was after me. In fact, I know he was after me because he made several passes even though he knew I was married. But anyway, we became friends, and even remained friends after my wife and I got an apartment in the western suburb of Melrose Park. His name was Fred and he lent me some money until I would receive my first pay check. My first priority with that money was beer, then cigarettes, and lastly food. After Betty and I had settled in Melrose Park, Fred would often visit. We had rented an upstairs studio apartment in an old neighborhood of Melrose Park, and I remember how the neighbors made it perfectly clear that they did not appreciate a black person anywhere near. I had come a long way; a long way in the wrong direction, and it wasn't long, and I was no longer going to school.

On July 16, 1966, my wife and I had a daughter and named her Maria Annette. Oh, what a beautiful Child. I was twenty. It was nine years after her Aunt Maria was murdered. But my daughter Maria would not hear about her Aunt Maria for another forty-six years.

On December 23, 1968, Betty and I were divorced. In 1970, acting against a court order, my ex-wife Betty left the state of Illinois to reside with our daughter Maria in the state of Michigan. How ironic; my sister Maria was taken from me by a kidnapper in 1957, and now in 1970, I put together and carried out a plan to kidnap my daughter Maria in Michigan. I succeeded and brought her back home to Sycamore. Her mother returned shortly after.

On March 22, 1971, I was drafted into the army, and it was about this time that my ex-wife Betty again took Maria to Michigan. In the summer of 1972 my daughter Maria visited with me while I was stationed in Washington D.C. I was assigned to the Pentagon. It was a good assignment. I worked for the Directorate of Military Support. The schedule was four days on then four days off; twelve hour shifts; two weeks days and then two weeks nights. You never really had time to get used to any routine, but you did have plenty of free time.

I remember that visit from my daughter as though it was yesterday. I remember so vividly how Maria held on to me crying as I said good-by to her on the plane. Little did I know that this would be the last time I would see her for forty years. Sometime afterwards they had moved and I knew not where. I was twenty six years old.

On September 29, 2011, at the visitation receiving line of my sister Kay's visitation, there she was, standing before me and needing to introduce herself to me as my daughter Maria. My sister Kay was my daughter Maria's Godmother. This was three months to the day that I was informed that they were about to arrest the person who had killed my sister Maria. I was sixty five years old.

During those forty years I had forced myself to no longer even allow thoughts of my daughter to enter my head. When those thoughts did occur, or when I was asked about her, those thoughts and questions where quickly brushed aside. I now had two painful memories of my beloved Maria's. I continued to drink daily. The thought of becoming a minister was a distant memory. I had remarried again, adopted my wife Georgia's two year old daughter Diane, and she became my own. I continued to drink daily, and in October of 1980, I left the industrial world of employment and purchased a country bar in Virgil, Illinois. It was eight miles east of Sycamore on Route 64. I remember, when my daughter Maria was only a few months old, I had a short lived life as a part time Electrolux Vacuum Cleaner salesman. At one time I had gone to this same bar attempting to sell a vacuum cleaner. I did not make a sale, but the owner was successful in his sale. He was successful in getting me drunk.

I named the bar Beak's Place, Beak being a nickname I received in high school. It was a family bar and we ran it as a family. My wife Georgia worked during the day and I worked during the night. Even my daughter Diane worked there on the weekends once she turned sixteen. It was here that I got sober and my life began to change once again.

In December of 1987 I had an aneurysm burst and I almost bled to death. The doctor told me that it was a result from prolonged alcohol abuse which had thinned the walls of my blood vessels. He told me point blank that if I continued to drink I would die. I was in the hospital for several days and the day I was released I went to my first AA meeting. I was forty one years old.

A very good friend of mine, a childhood friend from the neighborhood, from school, and from church, was one of the first people to visit me in the hospital. He knew I was an alcoholic and from time to time would causally ask me if I thought perhaps I was drinking a little too much. You see, he was not only a childhood friend but also a childhood drinking buddy. The difference was he had been given the gift of sobriety nearly twenty years earlier. It was this friend that took me to my first AA meeting, and has continued to be a guiding force in my life today. In my early sobriety, as I struggled with certain aspects of my past, he was the one that told me to just not go there. He pointed me to the positives and reminded me not to live in the past. He reminded me that the negative would lead only to the negative.

Alcohol had been so much a part of my life. Alcohol controlled me. And I thank God that I learned early on that if I thought about a drink for more than a second, that I would have that drink. There was no doubt in my mind. Therefore, whenever the thought of a drink entered my mind I had to immediately dismiss it. Literally, I had to shake my head, an instantaneous action, as though I could actually physically shake the thought out of my head. And this process has worked for me now for over twenty-eight years. That, and the support of people, along with regular attendance at AA meetings, has kept me sober.

At my first AA meeting I felt the presence of God. Please understand, I had never forsaken God. I had never stopped believing in God. I knew that God was always with me. But for so many years I lived surrounded by this alcoholic haze; this fog through which I viewed God. I had allowed alcohol to rob me of all that God wanted me to have. I am so thankful that from the very first I understood that if I were to live, I must live free from alcohol. And I turned to God, and he has delivered me.

With us is the Lord our God to help us and to fight our battles.
2 Chronicles 32:8

Prayer for deliverance

Almighty and Eternal God, I say you are almighty; let me know it, and let me trust it in my heart. Forgive me Lord for my lapses in total reliance upon your mighty hand. The kidnapping and murder of my sister Maria changed and influenced who I was. I have often looked for an easy way out. I turned to alcohol. I have gone in the wrong direction, as I was faced with another great loss, the loss of my daughter as well. Forgive me Lord. The painful memories are so great, and I turn less and less to you, and more and more to alcohol.

But now, Almighty and Eternal God, I see your hand. I have received your wake-up call. And as I lay there in the hospital, you send me just the right medicine. You send a true friend; a friend that has taken me by the hand to lead me in a new direction. And this friend continues to be a guiding force as your instrument in my life today. I praise you Almighty and Eternal God as you have helped me to fight my battles. I turned to you, and you delivered me. And now Almighty God, I pray for your almighty hand to continue to fight my battles. I pray for your continued deliverance. I pray for your help. Glory be to your name. Amen.

I again divorced on September 14, 1988, and my daughter Diane and I continued to operate the tavern. On July 18, 1993, I married again.

My wife Diane was the mother of one of my daughter Diane's best friends from high school. She was also the sister of one of my part-time bartenders, as well as an old classmate of mine.

The first step of Alcoholics Anonymous is this: "We admitted that we were powerless over alcohol and that our lives had become unmanageable." For years before I stopped drinking I knew that I was an alcoholic. I had no problem admitting it. It did not matter. I simply did not care. But once I did care, once I knew without a doubt that it meant living or dying, it did matter. At my first AA meeting I had no problem admitting before others that I was powerless over alcohol. However, it was a long time before I realized that my life had become unmanageable. That is how crazy alcoholism is. As I have just described for you a good portion of my life, how could anyone believe that it was not out of control, unmanageable?

> *The mind of sinful man is death, but the mind*
> *controlled by the Spirit is life and peace.*
> *Romans 8:6*

Prayer on allowing God to manage our lives.

Lord God, Father, Son, and Holy Spirit, how crazy my life has been as I took control! I am a sinner, and sin leads to death. But with you, my Triune God, there is life. I thank and praise you for your intervention. And I pray for your continued influence and guidance, and I pray for your Spirit to take control of that which I cannot, and grant me life, and peace. Amen.

With my sobriety came new life. It was not long after I had become sober, that my good friend once again gave me a little shove as he pointed me in another right direction. He said, "You know, it wouldn't hurt you to go to church." And I did. It was a mid-week evening service at my home church of St. John Lutheran in Sycamore, Illinois. And I cried as the Lord welcomed me. Soon after, I renewed old friendships; childhood friendships with some of those who were closest to me when Maria was kidnapped. I also reached out to some of my classmates when I was studying for the ministry, one of which was Reverend Paul Koester from West Allis, Wisconsin. Paul was the guy who replaced me in the starting lineup when I was kicked off the basketball team for drinking. He also delivered the message of comfort and assurance at Maria's re-burial service on July 22, 2012.

In the fall of 1994 I went back to what had now become Concordia University Wisconsin to again study for the ministry. God had changed my path and there I was, not even knowing where it would take me. In 1997 I sold the bar, and in 1998 I was installed as Deacon of my home church of St. John in Sycamore. My entire family was there, everyone except my two Marias.

In 2001 I became the director of Christian Senior Ministries, a mission ministry to the nursing homes and senior residence facilities in Dekalb and Ogle counties. This was a ministry which I founded with the help of the Reverend George E. Krause of the Immanuel Lutheran Church in Dekalb, Illinois. This was all God's doing. I had been a slave to alcohol. Alcohol had isolated me from all that God wanted me to have. I never stopped believing in him or loving him, but alcohol had surrounded me with this haze, this barrier. I could still see God, but only dimly. God delivered me from slavery. Yes, he used others as his instruments, but It was his doing. It was his power.

Though we are slaves, our God has not deserted us in our bondage.
Ezra 9:9

Prayer of thanksgiving for deliverance.

Gracious Lord and Father, you see and know all things; Father you know best how to help me. But I know little if anything. I am often blinded by dark clouds and hazes that surround me. It seems that I often turn to anything except you and your word. I have isolated myself from all that you want me to have. I can see you Lord, but only dimly because I have removed myself from your presence. Forgive me.

Gracious Lord and Father, I thank you for putting people in my life to offer good advice. I thank you Lord for bringing me back into your fold. I thank you Lord for giving me expectations. I thank you Lord for bringing me closer to you.

Gracious Lord and Father, now I pray for your continued intercession as you come to me in your Living Word, and as you send messengers to help and advise me. I pray Lord that you continue to move me closer to you and your peace and deliverance. In Jesus Name. Amen.

The first day of Jack McCullough's trial I walked into that court room and there in the front row of seats sat my daughter Maria. I cried. On the last day of the trial, my granddaughter Taylor, who was fourteen years old and interested in the legal system was there with her mother Maria. Maria thought it would be good for her to see our justice system in action. Taylor knew little about me, and little about her Ridulph heritage, but during closing arguments she cried. Maria said she never cries, but on that day, listening to what had happened to her great aunt, she cried.

Over the years, and especially since the trial, many people have shared with us their thoughts on how Maria's kidnapping and murder had changed their lives. Many told of how this tragic event changed the way we lived here in Sycamore. As I look back over the years, I am well aware of how it impacted my life and who I now am. But I don't think I realized those changes as much as others did. Perhaps since the impact affected us greatly as a family, we just were not aware of the more subtle changes in our life style.

Now, what I do remember so vividly on that first night was when a friend of mine, Kelly George, who was later killed in a tragic accident, had come to our front door and asked if I could come out and again join the search for Maria. My mother said this: "I have lost one child tonight.

I am not going to lose another." And as I think about it now, I have to wonder if perhaps that might have played a role in my parents decision, only three years later, of allowing me to go off to a private prep-school, a school in which I was so closely guarded by leaders of the church.

Also, now as I look around, I don't see children playing unaccompanied by an adult as was the common practice in 1957. We now carry keys to our homes. Our children know what it means to lock a door, and not talk to a stranger. Even my eleven year old grandson Keegan, the same age I was when Maria was kidnapped, is not allowed to walk to school alone. And he lives only three blocks from the same West School that Maria and I attended. My wife Diane goes with him.

Recently I was discussing this with my daughters Diane and Maria when asked if I was overly protective with Diane when she was little. I said no. But Diane quickly corrected me. She remembers vividly of being reminded of what could happen; of what did happen to her Aunt Maria.

This time from the very beginning has been a horrible experience for us. From the time that State's Attorney Clay Campbell and Detective Dan Hoffman came to my home to tell us that they had found the person responsible for my sister Maria's murder until now has been a great burden to say the least. It has been overwhelming, and my every thought was intermingled with thoughts of my little sister. When I prayed, when I tried to sleep, when I slept, when I awoke, when I worked, when I played, she was constantly in my thoughts.

My family was a great source of comfort, however, my sister Maria and this tragedy was overwhelming. Then the miracle happened. My Daughter Maria whom I had not seen in forty years was suddenly standing before me at my sister Kay's funeral visitation. She had been taken by her mother when she was only five. Now new thoughts flooded my mind; thoughts of wonder, thoughts of guilt, anger, uncertainty, and joy. And after that night of September 29, 2011, my sister's visitation, my mind continued to be flooded with thoughts of Maria, two Maria's. And the thoughts of wonder, guilt, anger, and uncertainty, were now overshadowed with thoughts of joy. No, more than thoughts, but with the experience of joy.

God brought my daughter Maria back into my life because it is his will that a father and a daughter should embrace one another in a loving relationship. And God's timing could not have been better. This was all new to her, and I am certain at times confusing, yet she has been there by my side. Maria was there along with the rest of my family. I thank God that by his hand my sister Maria has found justice. And I thank God that by his hand my daughter Maria has come back to me. I thank God for the two Marias in my life.

My intercessor is my friend as my eyes pour out tears to God.
Job 16:20

Prayer on God's intercession

Lord God, my Heavenly Father, I cannot help but praise you. Maria's kidnapping and murder changed lives, it changed a town. From the very beginning it has been a horrible experience. It has been a great burden. It has been seemingly overwhelming, and at times it continues to be even today. But then a miracle happened, and that miracle continues to grow with your assistance. Lord God, Heavenly Father, as always your timing could not have been better. Joy has come to the forefront, and I pray Lord God, my heavenly Father, that you enable me to stay in that presence of joy. I pray Lord God that you enable me to grasp the joy and the peace which you so graciously give at the right time, and in the right manner. Amen.

You know, sometimes we are just not ready to hear certain words of promise from the Bible. Now that is certainly sad, but I am sorry to say is true. You see, often times a person is so full of grief, or anger, or guilt, or some other extreme emotion, they simply are unable to hear the promises which God gives us. At times like that we are just not ready to hear that it will be alright. We are not ready to hear that God will provide when at that very moment we are dealing with the fact that God did not provide; or so it seems. When you feel that you or your loved one was forsaken, how can you believe that our Lord will never leave you or forsake you? How can your hearts be open to the love of God? How can you find peace in the midst of turmoil? How can an embittered heart find joy?

When I was going through the instruction process of prison ministry, one of several things which really struck me was the section on the understanding of a father. We as Christians generally do not have a problem with the understanding of God as our heavenly Father. In the prison population however, many do. Many inmates in our prison system do not have a positive image of a father. Many only have experienced a father that has abandoned them; or raped them, or beat them. So, what do you do? Do you not use the reference of God the Father? How can we eliminate the powerful image which God has given of himself? Well, the first thing we have to do is do away with the false image!

Throughout this horrible chapter in our lives, my sister Pat and I have tried to reflect, have tried to reveal God's goodness. In knowing that in all things God works for the good of those who love him; in able to truly understand this, we too had to do away with the false image. You see, once again it is so important to keep things simple. In order to find the good you must first recognize the source of both the good and the evil. That's right. All good things come from God, and all that is bad comes from the Devil. God can do, or will, no evil; only good! This is absolutely import to know if you are to understand that in all things God works for the good of those who love him. This is all important for you to know so that you can do away with the false image. You need to keep it simple!

God did not will for my sister Maria to be kidnapped, raped, and murdered. That is impossible since God can do or will only do that which is good. God did not plan or do this or any other evil thing. All evil is the result of sin. All that is bad comes from sinful thoughts, or sinful conditions created by people.

Many times, perhaps every time tragedy strikes, we need someone or something to blame. And even when we do not think we are blaming God, we in reality are as we ask these questions. "Where were you God?" "Why did you allow this to happen?" "Why didn't you protect them?" It is at this time when we need to know, I mean really know, that God did not, nor could not, have willed or brought about the tragedy!!! Sin is the cause. A sinful man did this evil thing. Now, knowing that, and knowing that in spite of that, knowing that in all things God works for the good of those who love him, you need to expect, to anticipate, to look for the something good which is to come out of it.

You need to expect, to anticipate. You need to look for the something good which is to come out of it. Now, I have said it twice, but does that mean you are ready to do this? Most likely no; not at first. In the beginning you are just overwhelmed with the pain. So, what do you do? Where do you turn? You turn to God. You turn to his Word. You turn to the people he has placed in your life. You focus on God's promises. You have seen what he can do, now trust him.

He does not ignore the cry of the afflicted.
Psalm 9:12

Then they cried to the Lord in their trouble,
and he saved them from their distress.
Psalm 107:13

Prayer getting beyond the pain.

O Father of Mercies and God of all Comfort, I have heard your promises, and I have seen what you have done. I have seen that not one word has failed of all the good promises you gave, and in this I find comfort and strength. But Father, I must confess that sometimes my heart is not open to your love. Sometimes I wonder how I can find peace in the midst of turmoil. How can my embittered heart find joy? Father forgive me. Let me see your true image as my loving and merciful Father, the God of all comfort.

O Father of Mercies, allow me to clearly understand that you can do no evil but only good. O Father of Mercies, prepare me, allow me, bring me to the point where I can see beyond my pain, so that I can now search for that which is good. Enable me Father to turn to you, my father which art in heaven, and to focus on your great promises. Enable me, Father of Mercies, to trust in you. In and through my Lord and Savior Jesus Christ I pray. Amen.

God has promised us; God wants for us that which is good. And you know what? As you strive to get beyond the bad, the light of the good begins to shine through, especially if you are anticipating it. My sister Pat and I embraced each other as never before. Our families rallied around us. Friends from whom we had not heard for years, even decades, reached out to us. Even strangers from near and far offered words of comfort and prayers.

Shortly after the announcement that an arrest had been made for the murder of my sister, I was at Maria's grave, when a man and woman walked up to me. They were from the far north side of Chicago and had driven two hours to visit Maria's grave and to pray for us. They had read about it in the paper and felt compelled to come. Childhood friends and neighbors that had long moved away contacted us. Distant relatives from here and overseas contacted us. Those who had lived through that horrible night in 1957 along with us, and those that had just heard about our terrible loss contacted us. God brought them and their love to our aid. God fulfilled his promise to never leave us or forsake us.

After the trial I offered a letter of thanks which was published in the Dekalb Daily Chronicle. It reads in part as follows:

"On Friday, September 14, 2012, Jack McCullough was found guilty of the kidnapping and murder of my sister Maria. Maria was only seven years old when she and her friend Kathy were innocently playing near our home. On December 3, 1957, nearly 55 years ago, Maria was taken from us, and after the verdict was given I was asked how I felt.

Today, in front of the Sycamore fire and police departments stands a plaque which reads, *"This is in memory of Maria Elizabeth Ridulph who on December 3rd, 1957, was kidnapped while playing near her home. She was found murdered in the spring of 1958. This is also in honor of the great people in our community that reached out with their love and compassion."* And today, as I look back over the events of the past fourteen months, I again wish to thank the great people in our community that reached out with their love and compassion. In fact, not only to those in our community, but also to the many family members, friends, and strangers throughout the country who have shared and supported us throughout this difficult time.

In December of 1957, my family received the love and compassion of an entire community, and the same has held true today. I want all of you to know what that says about our community, in fact about the world in which we live. Jesus said, *"I tell you the truth, whatever you did for one of the least of these brothers of mine, you did for me." Matthew 25:40.* All of you, by your thoughts, your prayers, and your presence, have helped myself and my family through this most difficult of times. Maria left us after only seven short wonderful years, but her memory lives ever so brightly, not only in the hearts of my sister Pat and myself, but also in the heart and soul of this community.

At the trial I met a couple from DeKalb, after seeing them there day after day, I asked who they were and if I should know them. They said, "Oh no. We have only lived here for a few years, but we just want to be here to show you our support." I met another young woman who was relatively new to Sycamore and she was very much interested in the history of the town in which she lived, and to her this trial was a part of Sycamore's history. Yesterday, I visited Maria's grave. There were placed flowers, stuffed animals, and other gifts for a child. I was surprised. But

I should not have been. Yes, I express my thanks to the great people in our community that reached out with their love and compassion."

I went on to say, "Jack McCullough has finally been brought to justice, and as we await his sentencing we are thankful that this part of our lives is now behind us. We are also thankful that with this conviction comes hope to so many others who still seek answers and justice in cases which may have seemed forgotten. With the successful arrest, prosecution, and conviction of the person responsible for taking my sister from us over a half century ago, I know that elsewhere, old, sometimes forgotten crimes will receive new looks. And for that, I am thankful."

Since the arrest and conviction of Jack McCullough there have been many old cases which have received a new look by authorities. I am convinced that the successful prosecution of our case, which was fifty-five years old, the oldest cold case every prosecuted in America, has encouraged this trend.

On Friday, January 22, 2016, an editorial was published in the Dekalb Chronicle in response to a full page ad soliciting information concerning the disappearance of Bradley Olsen. This young man disappeared in January of 2007. The editorial said, "We're just waiting for that one person to tell us where he's at," Susan Olsen said, "or to have a guilty conscience and tell us everything." One day it will happen. It happened for the family of Maria Ridulph, when Jack McCullough's mother finally told her family that she'd lied way back in 1957 to protect her son."

You see, God does not go back on his promises. It is true that their fulfillment does not always come to us in the form which we anticipate. In fact, they seldom do. But know this, God will only give us good things. Yes, even in the midst of the trials we may face, God will give us good things. Through Maria's tragic death many others are now given hope and comfort. And, this is only the beginning. The Bible tells us, *"We know that in all things God works for the good of those who love him." Romans 8:28.*

Prayer on seeing the good.

Gracious Lord, God of all Mercies, I thank and praise you for who you are. I have seen the light of your goodness as it shines through the darkness. I have seen the fulfillment of your promises, not only from past mercies, but also right now in my insignificant life. And now I thank you that I am able to anticipate that which is good. I thank you, Gracious Lord, as you have brought so many along with their love into my life, giving me aid in the fulfillment of your promise to never leave me or forsake me. I thank you Lord for showing me that you do not go back on your promises. And now I pray that you enable me to see that this is only the beginning. I pray that you enable me to trust that you will indeed give me good things. Amen.

As a child did you every play a game where you would spin around over and over, faster and faster, until you were at the verge of falling down? It was as if your mind was scrambled wasn't it? Well, that is how it was. And I think we have all experienced it at one time or another. In 1957, my sister Kay said, "Our minds were running out of control." And I said, "My mind was swirling." And then, in 2011, fifty-four years later, I wrote, "It is hard to think of anything else; even in my dreams!"

The weeks following the arrest of Jack McCullough for the murder of my sister Maria were dominated with bad thoughts. Even in my prayers I could not escape them. I would go about my daily life, but in everything, in every aspect, thoughts of Maria and what had happened to her took over. Everything seemed to get drowned out, even the good was overshadowed with this evil. It was then, when I needed it most, that God brought something new to light. No. Not something new, but something dramatic, something extreme. You know how it is. Sometimes we just need divine intervention in bringing us back from that dark place that surrounds us.

My sister Kay had been undergoing regular chemotherapy treatments for cancer for over seven years. On September 25, 2011, she was relieved of her pain to enter eternal bliss with our Lord in heaven. Three days later, at her visitation which was held in the church sanctuary, we were comforted by the presence of so many loved ones and friends. My sister Pat and I stood along with Kay's three boys: Larry; Lynn; and Lee, as we greeted the visitors. As I was greeting someone, I noticed my sister Pat hugging a young lady. Pat was crying. I continued talking with the guest before me as Pat took hold of my arm. She asked if I knew who this was, referring to the pretty young woman. I said, "She looks familiar, but no, I don't recall who she is." Pat said, "This is Maria."

I was shocked! I was speechless. The only thing I could say is "Can I huge you?" She said yes, and I just did not want to let her go. I was shaking. It was a brief encounter, and she moved on to greet Kay's boys, her cousins, saying, "I'm Maria, Chuck's daughter." To this very moment that was one of the greatest things I ever heard. But it came as a great surprise to us. We just did not know how to react. Next, at Pat's direction, Maria and her husband, whom we hardly noticed, went over to introduce themselves to Pat's daughter Theresa and son Mike. I stood there frozen, just watching. I watched as she left the sanctuary and paused at the picture display boards in the church lobby. Thank God she did not just leave before I regained at least some of my senses.

I excused myself from the visitation line and went to the lobby to talk to Maria. I asked her if they were going to be here for the funeral the next day. She said no, that they had to get home to their children. I then asked if it would be OK for me to contact her, asking if she would leave her address in the guest book. She said that she would. I returned to the reception line to continue greeting the visitors, but I continued to watch Maria as she spent some time viewing the photos of Kay and her family. When I saw her leave I took the first opportunity to go and see if she did in fact leave her contact information. I searched the book and could not find it. I looked again to see if I had somehow missed it, but found nothing.

Needless to say my mind was going a thousand miles a minute for the rest of the visitation. When the visitation was over, I checked the registration book one more time…just in case. I was totally disappointed, but I guess not really surprised. It had been so many years, and who knows what stories she had been told about me. That evening after the visitation, as I sat with close friends and family, the conversation was of course about how Kay would be missed. The conversation was also about my sister Maria's murder case, but mostly about my daughter Maria. I could not help but think that I must have disappointed her by my reaction to her being there. What did I say? What could I have said? What should I have said?

An anxious heart weighs a man down.
Proverbs 12:25

Anxiety prayer

Lord God, Creator of all things, you made me and all things to be good and well pleasing in your sight. We, I, by my sin, changed all of that. But in your great love you have restored all things in Christ Jesus. Lord God, I continue to sin. I have often failed to do the things which I should, and have done the things which I should not have done. And for that I ask forgiveness, and I rejoice in the forgiveness which is mine in Christ.

Lord God, Creator of all things, my mind was scrambled, out of control. My mind was dominated by bad thoughts. I was again being confronted with the horror of my sister Maria's murder, and now I was grieving over the death of my sister Kay. But in the midst of that, you brought something new to light. In the midst of my shock and confusion you again created something new, something good, for me. I thank you Lord, and I pray that you continue to replace my anxiety with the joy of something new, the joy which is found only in you, my Lord God, and my Creator. Amen.

It was late when I got home that night, and I was in this sort of daze. I could not sleep. My thoughts were going from wonder, to anger, to guilt, and again to wonder. I was angry at Maria's mother for taking her away from me. I found myself again angry at my sister Kay for never

75

letting me know that she had been in contact with my daughter when she was still a child. I found myself again feeling guilt about perhaps not doing all that I could to find her over the years. My mind and my emotions were racing.

The next day, the day of the funeral, the first thing I did was again go through the registration book to see if somehow I had missed her address. Not finding anything, my hope became that maybe she just needed a little more time before she decided if she wanted me to contact her. My mind, my heart was about to burst. I was grieving the loss of my sister Kay, whom I dearly loved. I was again grieving the loss of my sister Maria. And I was wondering if I had again lost my daughter Maria.

But you, O God, do see trouble and grief;
You consider it to take it in hand. The victim commits himself to you.
Psalm 10:14

Prayer on turning it over to God

Lord God, my heavenly Father, you see all. You consider it and take it in hand. I on the other hand cannot. I often live in a daze. My mind and my heart are about to burst as I grieve my losses. Help me! Help me Lord to do as you call me to do; help me to turn away from my uncertainty and my grief. Help me to turn to you.

Lord God, my heavenly Father, as I pray to you for help and deliverance, let me trust that you will hear my prayer. Lord God, as I turn my cares and my woes over to you, let me leave them there. Lord God, let me trust that you will take it in hand. Amen.

Kay's funeral and the sharing with family and loved ones came to an end, and shortly after we had arrived home, my nephew Larry called me and asked if I could come over to his house. He said that he had something for me. He had found an envelope in the memorial box with Maria's address on it. I couldn't get out there fast enough. "Oh ye of little faith!" I thought.

In my journal I wrote, "Kay died on September 25, a blessing, but she will be dearly missed. I am surprised how well Pat is actually taking it. I was really worried about her. At her visitation my daughter Maria was there. What a shock that was! Between the events with my sister Maria, Kay's death, and now struggling with my daughter Maria suddenly appearing, it has been the most difficult time of my life. But I have been praying constantly and trust that God's will will be done and this has changed turmoil into peace."

The theme in my journal for November 30, 2012, read: "They that trust the Lord find many things to praise him for. Praise follows trust." I wrote, "WOW! Praise follows trust! Had to stop and think about it and glad that I did! Trust brings results, and results command praise! The sentencing hearing was rescheduled today because of a technicality. Disappointing as we hoped for this to be over." Well, it is certainly true that trusting in the Lord will create many things to praise him for. I need to remember that, and so do you.

Jesus said, "You of little faith, why are you so afraid?"
Then he got up and rebuked the winds and the
waves, and it was completely calm.
Matthew 8:26

Prayer on Trust

Gracious and good Lord, you have revealed yourself to me; you have shown me your goodness. And yet I often struggle with doubt. Forgive me. This has been a most difficult time in my life. I have turned to you knowing that you are gracious and good, and then I worry. Where is my faith? Forgive me Lord. Enable me Lord, to pray with expectation. Enable me Lord, to pray with patience. Enable me Lord, to pray with the knowledge that you rebuked the winds and the waves, and it was completely calm. Enable me Lord, to trust the same for me. Enable me to trust that you will also rebuke the winds and the waves in my life, and that you will bring to me the complete calmness that only you can give. Amen.

Kay's funeral was on a Friday, and the next day I sat down to write to my daughter Maria. Where would I begin? So much I wanted to say! I wanted it to be just right.

The letter was long and hand written. I mailed it on October 3, 2011. I wrote, "It was a real shock to see you just standing there right in front of me. Even now my mind is just racing with thoughts. Before the visitation the thought crossed my mind that you might be there, just as it did when my dad died and then again when my mother died. But as always I quickly dismissed that thought. Oh how I wish you could have gotten to know my parents, your grandparents before they died. Even in you absence you were very special to them." I then went on to tell her, "I feel so deep within me a love for you which I cannot explain; a love which for so many years I have not been able to focus on because it was too painful." I tried to explain the void which her absence had left. I told her of my love. I told her how the whole family loved her. I told her we wanted to welcome her home.

So I made up my mind that I would not
make another painful visit to you.
For if I grieve you, who is left to make me
glad but you whom I have grieved?
2 Corinthians 2:1

I had lost my daughter Maria and it grieved me. Over the years I dealt with that grief by not allowing myself to think of her. That is how I coped; right or wrong. Now, after all those years I was able to hold her in my arms, even if only briefly. I never wanted to let her go again. I wanted nothing more than to have my daughter back. God, in his infinite power and wisdom, revealed to me that that void which her absence had left in my life, could only be filled by her. It was not God's will for us to be separated. The pain which I was experiencing should not lead me to surrender. I praise God, I thank him for the fact that Maria had the courage to stand there and say, "I'm your daughter." God had brought us together once again, face to face. Now, no longer, under any circumstances, would I be guilty of blocking her out. Yes, *"Who is left to make me glad but you whom I have grieved?"* Now I prayed, and I waited.

Praying and waiting had to become major factors in my life. They should be major factors in all of our lives no matter what the circumstances may be. And you know what? When we pray we must believe. I mean really believe that not only does God hear our prayers, but that he also answers them. Yes, he answers them. And not only does he answer them, but he always answers them in a way which is far better than we ever expected.

The Lord has heard my cry for mercy; the Lord accepts my prayer.
Psalm 6:9

Prayer: God please continue your intercession.

O Eternal God, Merciful Father, I lost my sister Maria, my mother, my father, and my sister Kay to death, and it grieves me. I had lost my daughter Maria in part due to my own shortcoming. But now you have brought her back to me, and I am afraid that I may once again lose her. My mind is racing. The void which her absence left is huge. It is filled with pain. But, O Eternal God, Merciful Father, I know your will. I know that it was not your will for us to be separated, and this gives me strength. I thank you!

O Eternal God, Merciful Father, I pray for your continued intercession, and I wait. I pray and I believe. I believe, and yet I continue to worry. Forgive me. Enable me Lord, to continue in prayer trusting in your intercession no matter what the circumstances may seem to be. Fill the void within me. Fill it with your presence. Fill it with the certainty that your will for a father and a daughter to live together in love will be done. Amen.

We as Christians pray "Thy will be done". And yet, we so often act as if we don't know what his will is for us. Several weeks ago I was talking with someone who was going through a difficult period in her life, and the conversation led to the discussion of knowing God's will. Well, I am often asked about knowing God's will. I often hear, "I just wish that I knew what God would have me to do!" And I bet that all of you have heard, or perhaps even asked questions like this yourselves. Yes. What is God's will for me?

Well, what do you think about when you think of the will of God? I think that it is true that all of us, believers in Christ, and non-believers as well, do in fact think about the will of God at some time or another. And I think that people look at God's will differently at different stages in their lives, especially at different stages in their faith life. I think that all us seek to know God's will for us and for the lives of those that we love. But I also think that we make it so difficult. We approach our search for God's will as if it were something that he had hidden from us, as if he did not want us to know. But that doesn't make any sense does it? No. God wants us to not only know his will for our lives, but to also follow that will. Therefore, he makes it easy for us to see, and then he leads us by the hand according to that will.

My sister Kay, whom I dearly loved, would seek God's will on everything. She would practice what she called "fleecing", a term which you may be familiar with. It comes from the Bible, in the Book of Judges, when Gideon tested God by placing a fleece of wool on the ground through the night. If it remained dry while the ground around it was covered with dew he would know God's will. Well, as much as my sister loved the Lord, I could never convince her that looking for proof or signs to confirm God's will was not pleasing in God's sight. I suggested to her that it was simply a lack of faith that God would do that which is good. You see, God's will is much different than ours. His will is never wrong or faulty. His will is always right and leads us along the paths of righteousness.

I often talk about God's will. I often talk about it because it often comes up. So many think God's will is beyond us. And when I say that knowing God's will is easy, I am often looked at as though I am crazy. But you know we pray "Thy will be done", not "Reveal your will". You see, God has already revealed his will for us so clearly in his Living Word, in Christ Jesus. So the hard part is not knowing his will, but in trusting that his will will be done.

What I have said, that will I bring about;
what I have planned, that will I do.
Isaiah 46:11

Prayer on recognizing God's will.

Our Father which art in heaven, I praise and thank you for so clearly revealing to me all that I need to know about your will for me in Christ Jesus. I praise and thank you that you have done all that is necessary for your will to be done. Yet, often I act as if I don't know what your will is. Often I think and act as if your will has been lost. I try, and I search, I rationalize and I connive to mold in my mind what I think your will should be. Heavenly Father, forgive me.

My Father which art in heaven, you have told me that your will is much different than mine. It is never wrong or faulty. It is always right and seeks a perfect end. And I thank you for that Father, since my will is often flawed and self-serving.

Father, the hard part is not in knowing your will, but in trusting it will be done. I pray that you enable me to recognize your will as you have revealed it to me in your Living Word. I pray that you most of all enable me to trust in the fact that your will will be done. In Christ Jesus. Amen.

I have always believed in God. I always knew that God was almighty. I always knew that God was with me. I always trusted God. But the trust that I had in God for most of my life, although it was great, was nothing compared to the trust in God that I came to know and rely upon after my daughter Maria came back into my life.

In 2011 my life was turned upside down. Thank God I was sober! Thank God for his ever presence! Thank God for family, loved ones, friends, and strangers alike that he placed in my path! Thank God for his Word which he placed in my heart! Jesus taught me to pray "Thy will be done." Now if I can only believe it to be true.

Help me overcome my unbelief!
Mark 9:24

Prayer: Help me overcome my unbelief.

Most Righteous and Ever-Living God, I thank you for giving me my faith in you and what you have done for me in Christ Jesus. I thank you for continuing to increase in me that faith. And, at the same time, I ask for your forgiveness when my faith falters.

Most Righteous and Ever-Living God, you have instilled within me a trust in you that I have come to know and rely upon. And yet, my faith at times falters. I pray, Lord, that you help me overcome my unbelief. Amen.

In April of 2015 I delivered this message in part at the Trinity Lutheran Church in Hampshire, Illinois. I began with these few brief proclamations from the Bible. In the Gospel we hear, "Everything must be fulfilled." In the Book of Acts we are told, "Why does this surprise you." In the Epistle we hear, "Do not let anyone lead you astray." And in the Psalm, "The Lord will hear when I call to him."

I continued by saying, that these brief glimpses into God's Word led me to the topic of trust; maybe because trusting the Lord has been such an important part of my life over the past several years. As I may have shared with you before, I have always trusted in God; there has never been a time in my life when I didn't. But in comparison to the trust I now have in the Lord, it is as though I didn't have any trust in him before. And let me tell you, what a difference that has made in my life!

To trust or not to trust, that is the question. And the decision that is made between those two choices is what either gives you peace of mind, or makes you worry. Yes, worry from worry to worry your whole life through!

Jesus tells us, "Do not worry about tomorrow, for tomorrow will worry about itself. Each day has enough trouble of its own." (Mt 6:34) Well, we might say to that, as we often do, "I hear what Jesus is saying, but what about the "what ifs"? You know, what if this, that, and the other thing that might happen tomorrow? Yes, what about the "what ifs?" Well, the Bible says let the what ifs, worry about the what ifs! Well, that sounds like a fabulous idea, doesn't it? And that's exactly what every believer should do. But it's a completely different story when it comes to our troubled lives. Yes, we may pray for God's help, for his deliverance, but do we truly, no even more than that, do we totally believe, do we totally trust that God will come through?

You know it is so easy to say we believe in God. We hear it all the time don't we? But simply believing in God is no good to us. We have to know who God is and what he has done for us. We are to have faith, but faith in what? You have to believe that God can and will do all that he has promised, and then you must trust in those promises. You must know beyond any doubt that trusting God makes sense. It is like I recently told my confirmation class as I said the word faith can be comforting but misleading at the same time. You see, faith is only good if it is placed in that which is trustworthy. Faith must be placed in that which can be trusted beyond any doubt. And when you have that kind of trust let me tell you, it makes a difference. Yes, it makes a difference if you trust in God with your whole heart and put your entire life into his hands.

Somewhere I once read that trusting God is practical. Did you hear that? Trusting in God is practical. Well, when I first read that I simply had to stop and think about it. And as I did, the more sense it made.

Webster's Dictionary defines trust as an assured reliance on another's integrity, veracity or justice; assured anticipation or confident hope. This statement of trusting God is practical has really opened my eyes to the benefits, the blessings, which God so graciously wants us to have. It simply makes sense to trust in God. It is practical. I can rely upon God because of who he is, what he has promised, and what he is able to do.

Is it easy? No. Can it be done? Yes. Where do we begin? Well, first of all the Bible tells you very clearly that you cannot rely upon, you cannot trust in your own intellect or reasoning. Just look where that led Adam and Eve. And yet, we just do not seem to learn do we? We continue to put our trust in ourselves and in others. And you know what, sometimes that is not a bad thing, to a certain point. But let's be realistic; let's be practical. Our human history when it comes to issues of trust fall far short do they not? Like Adam and Eve, I too would have been tossed out of the Garden of Eden a long time ago simply because, left to my own devises, I am not trustworthy. And yet I continue to rely upon myself. I so often fail to turn to my almighty God and place my trust where it has proven to belong. It just does not make sense.

We say that God is almighty, that God is all-knowing, that God's will will be done. We say that God will never leave us, that God will take care of us, and yet, we often turn to our own ways or the ways of others. Over and over again in the Bible when the people followed God they prospered. But over and over when they went their own way, when they turned to false gods and their own devices, they suffered. And you know what? I don't have to look that far. I see in my own life the results of not trusting the Lord. And yet, why am I often so slow in learning? Why am I so foolish? Why am I so stubborn? Why don't I simply trust the Lord?

Well, the Bible tells us all that we need to know about trusting and leaning on our almighty God. My confirmation verse says it so clearly, "Not one word has failed of all the good promises he gave." (1 Kings 8:56) Yes. "Not one word has failed of all the good promises he gave."

So let me ask you, if that is true, which it has proven to be over and over again, then why in the world would you not trust him?

I want you to see it as I have seen it. Trusting God is not always easy because it simply goes against our human nature, but what I have discovered has made it workable for me.

First, determine just what God's will is for you in any given circumstance. How do you do that? Simply by seeing what he has revealed to you in his Word. Don't make it difficult, just keep it simple. The turning point for me was when I came face to face with my daughter which had been lost to me for forty years. What do I do? What do I say? How do I do it or how do I say it? When do I do something? When do I not? As you can well guess, these are only a few of the many questions and feelings running through my mind. But then, after a great deal of prayer, along with a great deal of anguish, the Lord showed me very clearly what he had already revealed to me over and over again. God's will is that a father and a daughter live together in a loving relationship.

Now, knowing what God's will is, do I believe it will be done? Yes! But was I ready to trust that it would be done? Did I know that trusting God in this overwhelming circumstance was practical?

I prayed that God would restore my daughter and myself into the loving relationship that I knew he willed for us. And then, when I began to worry about it, I simply reminded myself that his will would be done, over and over and over again. Was that easy? No. Even while I was praying for God's help, I was thinking about what I could do to make my prayer come true. How foolish! I had to fight those thoughts. I had to trust totally in God. And each time, in each circumstance, his will was done. It was a God thing as my sister Pat would say. And with each success, with each answer to my prayer, my trust in the Lord grew, and I came to realize that trusting God was practical. And you know what? I now know without any doubt that this process can work in any given situation that comes my way. Yes, trusting God is practical.

Listen to what God has to say, "Everything must be fulfilled." (Lk 24:44) Yes, everything, not some things; everything. Must be fulfilled; must, not might, not maybe, but must be fulfilled.

Next, "Why does this surprise you?" (Ac 3:12) We have seen the evidence over and over again. Especially the greatest fulfillment of all time, as God so loved the world that he sent his only begotten Son that whoever believes in him shall not perish but have eternal life.

Then, "Do not let anyone lead you astray." (1 Jn 3:7) And, finally, "The Lord will hear when I call to him." (Ps 4:3) Yes, trusting in God is practical!

This is the message that I shared with that little congregation in Hampshire, Illinois, and this is the message I want to share with you. God has led me through it all; not my worry, not my intellect, not my will. God. It has been a God thing. Do I continue to struggle with my lack of total trust? Yes. But thank God it has become not only easier, but more natural. And the timing could not have been better. God so clearly showed me that he is trustworthy in answering my prayers concerning my daughter Maria, so why would I doubt that he is trustworthy in comforting me and my family in the horrible circumstances surrounding the arrest and trial of my sister Maria's killer? Yes. Trusting God is practical!

God is our refuge and strength, an ever-present help in trouble.
Psalm 46:1

Jesus said, "Do not let your hearts be troubled.
Trust in God; trust also in me."
John 14:1

Prayer on trusting God.

God of Mercy and of Truth, you have clearly told me not to worry about tomorrow for each day has enough trouble of its own. You have told me to not let my heart be troubled. You have told me to trust in you for you are my refuge and strength, an ever-present help in trouble. God of Mercy and Truth, I have seen the results of not trusting in you. Why am I so foolish? Why am I so stubborn? Why don't I simply trust in you? Often times I pray for your help, but I do not totally trust that you will come through. Often times I want to know your will but then do not recognize it when you reveal it to me. Often times I recognize it but then do not follow it. Forgive me Lord.

God of Mercy and of Truth, trust is an important part of my life, and I have seen the difference that it makes. I have seen that trust in you is useful. It makes sense. It is practical. It is measurable. It is real, and it is something that I can understand. Yet, often my thinking is madness. My understanding is weak, crooked, and unreliable. Forgive me Lord.

I pray to you, God of Mercy and of Truth that you would enable me to trust you with my whole heart, my whole life, and lean not on my own understanding. I pray that you will remind me over and over again that your will will be done. God of Mercy and of Truth, you have led me through all things, not my worry, not my intellect, and not my will, but you, O Lord. Now, I pray that you strengthen that trust which you give me as a blessing of my faith. Amen.

New Year's Eve, 2015, I had been asked to substitute for one of our circuit pastors in leading the Thursday afternoon worship service at the Oak Crest Retirement Center. This was a good distraction for me since only two days earlier the headline of the local DeKalb Chronicle paper read, *McCullough Returning to Sycamore for Hearing.* This news was very disturbing! It also caught me by surprise. The preparations for this service would help in refocusing my thoughts.

I began my message with these words: Here we are closing out one year and entering a new one; closing out one period of our lives and entering another. And how do we approach this? With joy? With sorrow? With indifference? I went on to say that we may very easily start out this New Year complaining about the fuss, the routine, the daily grind which can wear you down until you feel like you can't stand it any longer. And all of this is likely to blind us to the glory of what is actually happening as we enter a new day, a new year. I went on to say that we are liable to deafen our ears and close our hearts to the fact that our Lord is with us always; that our Lord has good things in store for us.

Jesus said, "He who has ears, let him hear."
Matthew 11:15

A cheerful heart is good medicine.
Proverbs 17:22

Jesus said, "He who has ears, let him hear." In other words, our Lord has given us the means to deal with whatever comes our way. Jesus said these words right after he had told John's disciples to tell John this: "Go back and report to John what you hear and see: The blind receive sight, the lame walk, those who have leprosy are cured, the deaf hear, the dead are raised, and the good news is preached to the poor." The Lord is telling us, you and me, that in spite of all this, in spite of the worst possible scenarios, we have been given the means to overcome.

Now we are told in the Bible that "A cheerful heart is good medicine." It is like a rain cloud in the spring. It brings with it a good crop. It brings with it new life. Yes, in spite of our circumstances, the Lord gives us the means, just as on that New Year's Eve the Lord redirected my thoughts. The Lord gave me a new direction. The Lord turned me to his word and his promises.

Prayer: Lord open my ears and my heart.

Lord God, my Father in Christ Jesus, you have over and over provided me with the means to overcome that which the Devil and the world throw at me. And I thank you. But sometimes they sneak up on me. Sometimes I am blinded to your glory. Sometimes I am led to close my ears and my heart to the fact that you are always with me. Sometimes I forget that you have only that which is good in store for me. Lord God, forgive me.

Lord God, my Father in Christ Jesus, lead me in the right direction. Open my ears and my heart. Enable me to re-focus my thoughts. Lord God, I pray that you help me to grasp the means to overcome which you so graciously provide. I pray, Lord God, that you give me that cheerful heart which is indeed good medicine for my body and my soul. Amen.

Well, I had not been home for too long after the service when my sister Pat called. She had lots of news she just couldn't wait to share. You see, I was kind of a substitute for my sister Kay. Pat and Kay would usually speak daily (at the least…often several times a day). Pat would generally only call me when she had been thoroughly frustrated with her conversation with Kay. She would say, "Kay drives me crazy. I just had to call you." Since Kay's death, I became a second choice, and a weak one at that. But I enjoy her calls, and I try to call her often to help fill the void which Kay's death has created for her. Pat has been a real blessing to me during these very difficult years.

Therefore encourage one another and build each other up.
1 Thessalonians 5:11

Prayer: Help one another.

Gracious and Holy God, you have done it all for me as you have made me your own in your beloved Son Jesus Christ. You have given me such simple instructions; to love you and to love one another. You have told me so simply and directly to encourage one another and build each other up. So why do I so often fail or neglect that which is so important and yet so simple? Forgive me.

You have put those so near and dear to me in my life so that we can love and embrace one another; so that we can encourage and build each other up. And it works Lord. It works when we simply follow your directions. Help me, I pray. Help me to embrace, and help me to be embraced by those that you have put in my life. Amen.

My conversation with Pat on that New Year's Eve day turned to Jack McCullough. She knew how upsetting it was for me that he had been granted a new hearing. The thing that troubled me most was not the fact that he was getting the hearing, this was part of the judicial process. But what troubled me was that the prosecutor's office was in reality promoting it. They were attempting to get the case against McCullough overturned. And even now I as I write these words my stomach is churning. It is so stressful; so hard to deal with.

Pat had just spoken to our cousin Gigi who was really upset about the recent turn of events. She could just not understand, as we could not, how the state's attorney could act in such a fashion. State's Attorney Schmack had made it clear that he agreed with the defense council that McCullough was innocent. We felt abandoned by the system. We did not know what to do. Gigi told Pat that we should contact our state representative and ask him to intervene on our behalf. Pat and I spoke for a long time, but our conversation ended in frustration, really not knowing what, if anything we could or should do.

The discerning heart seeks knowledge, but
the mouth of a fool feeds on folly.
Proverbs 15:14

Prayer: What should I do?

Almighty God, Ruler over all things, I need to submit to your rule over me. Almighty God, you have led me to pray over and over, so many times, the AA Serenity Prayer, "God grant me the serenity to accept the things I cannot change, the courage to change the things I can, and the wisdom to know the difference." But I am so often that fool that feeds on folly. I become frustrated. I often have a relapse of not knowing what to do or where to turn. Almighty God, Ruler over all things, forgive me. Turn me around. Point me back to you, the Ruler over all things.

Almighty God, Ruler over all things, you have shown me where to turn. You have shown me my foolishness. You have shown me your might. And I now turn to you. I pray that you reveal your rule over me. I pray that you instill within me the certainty that you are in control. I pray that you grant me that serenity that is mine in Christ Jesus. I pray that you relieve me of my foolish notions which lead only to folly. In Jesus Name. Amen.

Nearly immediately after I had hung-up the phone from my conversation with Pat, the phone rang again. It was Julie Trevarthen, one of the two primary prosecutors at the trial of Jack McCullough for the murder of my sister Maria. She started out the conversation very directly saying she was concerned with what was happening at the state's attorney's office with the case. She was not the first person to tell us this.

When McCullough submitted his first post-conviction petition, Richard Schmack called, informing us of the petition, and said that we could pick-up a copy at his office and asked if we could meet with him. The meeting was tense nearly from the very beginning. He made it clear the direction he was going, and I asked him directly why he was spending so much time trying to prove his innocence instead of replying to the errors in the petition. He immediately handed each of us a list of his responsibilities, obviously anticipating the question.

It did not take long and it became apparent that he was not well versed in the case. When questioned on his comments about pre-trial motions and rulings on the exclusion of FBI (police reports), he left the conference room looking for something to substantiate his claims, which I was certain were incorrect. When he left the room, I told my sister Pat and her husband Bill that I had had enough and I was leaving. She said, "You can't go! You have to stay." He returned unable to prove his point. When we did leave, we were upset. I was angry. I told my brother-in-law later that day that I had felt as if we had needed an attorney with us. He said, "That's funny. I felt the same way." How sad! Speaking with the state's attorney representing your interests and thinking that you needed an attorney. He later made it very clear to us that he did not represent our interests.

The hearing was set for October, 28, 2015, and my sister and I had an uneasy feeling about it. We were concerned about a new theory concerning the time frames pertaining to the events leading to the murder of my sister; time frames which had been thoroughly investigated by the Illinois State Police during their investigation. It is unfortunate that these time frames did not come up at trial because the defense chose not to present an alibi defense. I hated the thought of going through those new time frames and numerous police reports which we had been given, but felt I should do so. I had not gotten very far before I realized there were some real differences. The more I read, the more evident it became as to why the trial judge along with the panel of appeal judges had ruled that the police reports were not admissible as evidence. I was just sick.

Since that time the judge has ruled against the post-conviction petition submitted by Jack McCullough and has also questioned the validity of another petition filed by McCullough's trial appointed public defender Tom McCulloch (McCulloch not to be confused with McCullough). That petition was also denied. A third petition, one which is nearly identical to the first two is scheduled to be heard January 14, 2016.

We want to move on. But it just seems so hard! It is so easy to get trapped in it all. Part of me wants to just turn it all over to God and let things fall as they may. But something is also telling me that I need to take some action here. You know, God does give us minds and the ability to think things through. God does encourage us to act according to his will, trusting in his direction according to his Word. But, with that being said, I must recognize that more often than not, when I rely upon my own initiative, I am just getting in God's way.

A wise man listens to advice.
Proverbs 12:15

Prayer: Let me listen.

Gracious God, Father in Heaven, you spoke and it was, and it was good. But, we, I, spoiled it all. And you continue to speak, but do I listen? Forgive me, Gracious God.

I become upset. I become angry. I become more and more agitated. I want to move on, but it seems so hard. It is so easy to get trapped in all the turmoil, all that is going on around me, all that is being thrown at me. And I am ready Lord. Let me listen.

Gracious God, Father in Heaven, I pray that you enable me to follow your lead. I pray that you let me not get in your way. I pray that you let me listen. I pray that you grant me the gift of discernment. Enable me, Gracious God, to listen, and to heed your message before I act, and then, Lord, let me step forward with courage. Amen.

As soon as I had finished speaking with Julie, I called my sister Pat. She felt that we should listen to Julie and ask her to contact an attorney on our behalf. We don't know to what end this will lead us, but we both agreed that it might give us some peace of mind. When I had finished speaking with Pat I told my wife Diane that I thought the Immanuel Lutheran Church in DeKalb was holding a 5:00 early evening New Year's Eve worship service. My mind was not in a good place, and worship would do me good.

Pastor Ray Krueger led that worship service, and during his message he stressed that God had placed people and circumstances in our lives. People to encourage and lift us up, and circumstances to strengthen and equip us. We confessed our sins and received absolution. The service was small in attendance, and we all joined together in communion signifying that we are one in Christ Jesus. Pastor Krueger proclaimed, "The peace of the Lord be with you always." And then he bestowed God's blessing upon us. My mind, for now, was clear.

Do not be afraid or discouraged…For the battle is not yours, but God's.
2 Chronicles 20:15

Prayer: Do not be discouraged.

O Lord, my Refuge and my Strength, how you do provide! I was, as I often am, not in a good place. You led me by my hand into the fellowship of your Church so that I might worship you, O Lord, my Refuge and my Strength. And I thank you.

O Lord, I thank you for the people, as well as the circumstances, that you have placed in my life for my encouragement, and for my strengthening. I thank you for bestowing upon me that peace which is beyond my own understanding, and that is with me always. I pray that you relieve me of my fears and discouragement. I pray that you enable me to see and to understand that the battle is not mine, but yours, O Lord, my Refuge and my strength. Amen.

Last night I woke up at about 3:30 AM, and as it has often been over the past few years, I was unable to return to sleep. My mind was racing. It was Thursday, and I had a funeral message to prepare for Saturday. My daughter Diane and her husband Jeff were having some problems and I was fighting off the feeling of resentment towards my son-in-law. McCullough's next hearing was next week. I continued to go from a state of peace and joy, to a state of turmoil and darkness. What should I do? Where should I turn? It reminds me of the time the Israelites were about to be taken into bondage. All the Lord wanted was for them to turn to him, to turn away from their false God's, and he would deliver them. But where did they turn? They turned to Egypt for help. Do you believe it? After all that they went through at the hands of Egypt. After all the rejoicing over being delivered out of Egypt, and where do they turn? Not to God, the great Deliver, but to Egypt. And what about us? Where do we turn?

Be still, and know that I am God.
Psalm 46:10

Prayer on knowing God.

Unto Thee, Oh Lord, I turn for deliverance. I have gone from a state of peace and joy to a state of turmoil and darkness; a state of captivity. What should I do? Where should I turn?

"Be still, and know that I am God." Unto Thee, oh Lord, I place my trust for you have shown me who you are by what you have done. Lord, I need to look no further. I pray that you enable me to be still in the midst of the turmoil, in the midst of all the noise that swirls around me. Enable me to be still and know that you are my God. And, Lord, with that knowledge, with that certainty, I pray for your deliverance. Amen.

In Alcoholics Anonymous one of the first things you hear is known as the serenity prayer. It reads like this: *God grant me the serenity to accept the things I cannot change; courage to change the things I can; and wisdom to know the difference.* This prayer is generally recited at every AA meeting throughout the world. Pictures and plaques featuring this prayer are sold and distributed everywhere. People have it tattooed on their bodies. It seems like such a simple prayer doesn't it? But for me, I struggled with it for nearly the first twenty-five years of my sobriety. I just couldn't get it! And for a long time I didn't even realize it.

In Alcoholics Anonymous you hear from the beginning some statements like, "Keep it simple stupid!" Things which should come naturally to us but don't. It is so funny, or sad really, that I can council people about their faith, about knowing God's will, and trusting him. I can tell them, and expect them to understand that we are to keep it simple; that we are not to complicate it, and then I ignore the advice of others. Over and over from my first days of sobriety I would hear that you cannot change people, places, and things. I understood the words and the concept. But I guess I never really gave them much thought. I never really understood the reasoning behind the advice. I never even tied the importance of this statement with grasping the serenity prayer. You see, I thought I could influence or change people and even circumstances. I knew that I could not impose my will upon others. But, with that being said, I was going to die trying. It just doesn't make sense does it?

One night I was at an AA meeting and this guy was talking about the hard time he was having. He was miserable, and it was affecting not only his life but the lives of those around him. He was working on this project, and his mind and his heart just wasn't in it. He said, "I just had to walk away." He literally did walk away from his project, but what he really meant was he had to walk away from the troubling situation. He could not change people, places, or things. I finally received a glimpse of understanding. *God, grant me the serenity to accept the things I cannot change; courage to changes the things I can; and wisdom to know the difference.*

It has been twelve days since I spoke with Julie Trevarthen on the phone; ten days since she was going to call with information regarding a victim rights attorney to represent us. And you know what? I am OK with that. I know Julie and trust in her good intentions. There could be, and I am sure are, many reasons why she has not called. In two days we go to court and hear Jack McCullough's petition and the judge's rulings, or even perhaps told of a postponement. But it is surprising to even me that I am OK. I am content. There are certain things I simply cannot change. And accepting that brings with it a great deal of relief, something in AA that we like to refer to as serenity.

Do not be anxious about anything, but in
everything, by prayer and petition,
With thanksgiving, present you requests to God.
And the peace of God, which transcends all understanding,
Will guard your hearts and your minds in Christ Jesus.
Philippians 4:6-7

Prayer on peace.

O Lord God, I know that you love me, and I know that you will take care of me. This in itself is sufficient for me. I can now be content in all circumstances. Or, can I? Forgive me Lord, for I am not always content. Forgive me Lord, I am often anxious.

Lord God, I thank you for all that you have done for me. I thank you Lord, for the help I know is mine for all things to come. But I often falter. I pray with thanksgiving, as I ask that you relieve me of any anxious thoughts. I pray with thanksgiving, as I ask that you give me that peace which transcends all understanding. I pray with thanksgiving, as I ask that you guard my heart and my mind in Christ Jesus. Amen.

Chapter Five

The Healing

The trial of Jack McCullough for the murder of my sister Maria was drawing to a close. The question was starting to be asked, "What if he is found not guilty?" My sister Pat and I started thinking about, and talking about that possibility. We both initially said, "It doesn't matter." Just like my father had said years ago when presented with the theory that the murderer had been identified, "What difference does it make?" But you know what? It made a traumatic difference to the Tessier family when he was found not guilty for the rape of his sister Jeanne. When the verdict of not guilty was announced his sister Kathy nearly fainted as she cried out in anguish. Michelle Weinman, who courageously had testified against him, gasped for air and wept. His brother Bob lashed out in anger; "This is a travesty of justice", he said. State's Attorney Clay Campbell called it a miscarriage of justice, and said the verdict sent a terrible message to victims of sexual assault. It made a difference. And deep down I knew it would make a difference to me as well. I said that the important thing was for us all to know the truth, and it was. But still, I am not sure to what extent, but I do know that it would have made a difference if he had been found not guilty.

The closing arguments had been made, and now we awaited the verdict. Shortly before court was to reconvene for the judge's verdict, Detective Mike Ciesynski approached me in the hall of the courthouse. Mike was one of the detectives from Seattle that had aided with the interrogation of McCullough. He asked how I was doing, and said that we were lucky to have a state's attorney who had the courage to pursue such an old case. He said the chances of achieving a conviction in a fifty-five year old case were slim at best, but regardless he said, Clay Campbell, because he had the courage to do the right thing, has made it possible for the truth to be made known.

Somewhere along the way I asked myself "What if he is found not guilty?" I am not sure when, but I think it was during this time of waiting for the verdict. It was then that I began searching for something good which might come out of this thing. Something good not just for me, but more importantly for others.

Stand at the crossroads and look; ask where the good way is,
And walk in it, and you will find rest for your souls.
Jeremiah 6:16

Hate what is evil; cling to what is good.
Romans 12:9

Prayer: Lord show me the good.

Dear Heavenly Father, you are the source of all that is good. And yet I often find myself searching for that which is good. Forgive me. I often find myself searching for that which makes a difference. Forgive me, Heavenly Father. Lord, as I stand at the crossroads and look, let me see. Enable me, Heavenly Father, to cling to what is good. Enable me to cling to you, the Source of all that is good. Heavenly Father, help me to see the good, and cling to it. Heavenly Father, enable me to walk in it, so that I might find rest for my soul. Amen.

On Friday, December 14, 2012, the verdict came in. Guilty. This time, unlike at the conclusion of the rape trial, there was no weeping, at least in this Sycamore courthouse. Here the courtroom burst out in shouts of celebration. It reminded me of something you might have seen in an ancient Roman coliseum. But in the front row of that courtroom, in the seats occupied by my sister and myself, along with our families, there was no rejoicing. I felt only relief.

At the bottom of the page in my journal it said, "It's your faith that God will have on display as evidence of his victory." I wrote: "I never doubted he would be found guilty. I believe that my impact statement which they urged me to prepare helped me in the healing process. I made a statement to the press after the verdict. Pat & my granddaughter Taylor were by my side. Although some were celebrating, we were not. It had been a very difficult time. I am glad my parents did not have to go through it. During the process, along with being reunited with my daughter Maria, my faith and especially my trust in God grew beyond belief!"

The sentencing of Jack McCullough for the murder of my sister Maria was scheduled for December 3, exactly fifty-five years after he had kidnapped her. (It was later changed to December 10 due to some technicality in the paper work.) The state's attorney's office had requested that both my sister and I submit victim impact statements to be given to the judge prior to his sentencing decision. They stressed how such statements might have a real impact on the judge's decision. On November 16, 2012, I wrote in my journal, "Pat, Bill and I met with the state's attorney's office today in preparation for court and the sentencing of McCullough. We had many questions since Clay Campbell was defeated in his re-election bid. We were shocked and disappointed by his defeat. It was a good thing that we had that meeting since I was not aware of the importance of our impact statements."

The thought for the day on the next page of my journal read, "Live fully each moment of today. Trust God to let you work through it. He will give you all you need. Don't skip over the painful moment, even it has its important and rightful place." How appropriate! I wrote: "Preached all week on being thankful and worked on my impact statement. Both were healing!"

My impact statement to the judge read as follows:

Your Honor, first of all I give thanks to God for all that has happened since that June 30th Thursday of 2011 when I was first informed by States' Attorney Clay Campbell that they had determined who had kidnapped and murdered my sister Maria. I wish to thank you, Your Honor, for your gift of discernment and your fair and impartial judgment. I wish to thank all those who have worked so hard to bring us to today. But I especially thank God for his hand was clearly seen throughout these proceedings.

The past seventy four weeks have been very difficult to say the least for myself and my family. Not only have old wounds and painful thoughts been brought back, but they have been brought back with a vengeance. In fact it is so much more than revisiting dark places. Now a face, a face of someone we knew, has been forever etched in my mind of the person who did this evil thing so many years ago. I have been forced to hear and to think about how my little sister was so terribly and brutally snatched away to have her short life snuffed out and then discarded like a piece of garbage. And, as I say this, I must stop and weep. I can only thank God that my parents are not alive to have to go through this torment once again.

No one should have to bury their children. No one should have to wait months in agony to discover whether or not their little child is still alive. No one should be asked to identify their little child by a piece of clothing and a lock of hair. No one should have to be haunted with gruesome thoughts of how their little child was molested and murdered. No one should have to endure such a horrible thing.

Jack McCullough committed an evil act which has impacted the entirety of our lives; the lives of myself, my parents, my sisters, and my children. My mother lived to be 93 years of age, and my father 94. Both of them when they died stated they could not wait to be with Maria. All their lives they longed to be with their little daughter. My mother only days before her death had a dream, a vision perhaps, of being in heaven with Maria.

Jack McCullough committed an evil act which would define who we are. Normally a younger child would be referred to as her brother's little sister. But, from that December day of 1957, I have been referred to as Maria's older brother. Over these 55 years, there has never been a great time lapse when someone has not said to me, "Are you Maria's brother? Is it too hard for you to talk about it?" And then they would go on to tell me how Maria's kidnapping had affected their life in some particular way. Yes, Jack McCullough committed an evil act which changed our lives forever.

When you pronounced that guilty verdict I experienced no surprise since the evidence presented was unquestionable, especially the evidence which would have been presented had he chosen to get on the stand and attempted to plead his case on the basis of his so called alibi. There was no surprise to the guilty verdict, but there was no relief either. As the Ridulph family sat in that front row of the court room, there were no shouts of joy coming from our lips. The fact is I see no victory here. The fact is Jack McCullough has been convicted of kidnapping and murdering my sister Maria. The fact is Jack McCullough took this innocent little girl. The fact is Jack McCullough has left a hole where there should be none. He has left questions: Would she have excelled at music? How would I have scrutinized her first boyfriend? Where would she have gone to college? Who would she have married? How many children would she have had? What fun we would have had together? The answer to all these questions, and so many more, Jack McCullough snatched away. No. There is no victory here.

As you now consider the sentencing of Jack McCullough for this most vile of crimes, I ask that the verdict which you pronounce make a bold statement to all that we as a society will not tolerate such evil crimes against our children. I ask that you pronounce the maximum sentence allowed under the law; not out of revenge, but for justice, justice for Maria, and justice for our community.

No amount of punishment will undo the evil which Jack McCullough has done. No amount of punishment will ease the pain and suffering he has caused. No amount of punishment will bring Maria back. However, the maximum punishment does speak volumes. The maximum punishment says that we will protect our children, and that we will punish those who bring them harm. For years the people of this nation have considered this crime committed by Jack McCullough against Maria a capital offense; the most vile of crimes. And now I ask that your verdict show that this is indeed the case. I ask that the sentence which you pronounce shouts out with a clear voice that those who abuse and murder our children will be punished to the full extent of the law."

My sister Pat's statement was very different. I believe it reflected that she was in a better place than I in the healing process. It read as follows:

"Maria's oldest sister to John:

I first want you to know that when the verdict was given at the end of your trial, I was not among those cheering. I am saddened by everything that has happened. I believe that your soul is damned; not because of what you have done, but because of the God you believe in.

I want you to know that I have been and will continue to pray for you. You are three months older than I, and I will be praying for you until one of us dies.

To Judge:

Fifty five years ago John Tessier, now known as Jack McCullough, robbed me of my sister, Maria. I had another sister and we were best friends, sharing absolutely everything. I know that my relationship with Maria would have grown to be the same. I look through the pictures I have of her now, and I see how her life was so short. Judge, I recommend that you consider a sentence of fifty five years for the man that took her life."

Those were our statements.

I had said before the verdict was announced that the important thing for all of us was to know the truth. But you know what? I am not sure to what extent, but I do know that it would have made a difference if he had been found not guilty. In my impact statement made at the trial I thanked the judge for his gift of discernment and for his fair and impartial judgement. I said, "When you pronounced that guilty verdict I experienced no surprise since the evidence presented was unquestionable, especially the evidence which would have been presented had he chosen to get on the stand and attempt to plead his case on the basis of his so called alibi." I was told before the verdict was announced that regardless of the outcome, the trial made it possible for the truth to be made known. Now, today, nearly four years later, Dekalb County Judge William Brady reversed the guilty verdict of Jack McCullough for the murder of my sister Maria. This is what I had to say about the truth being made known:

It was stated in the court room that the fact is Maria Ridulph was abducted between 6:40-6:55 P.M. proving his innocence. This has been repeated on national TV network news as fact. And you know what? If there was even a hint of truth to this being the least bit credible, I would have been in support of Jack McCullough's release from prison. But the fact is this, based on those FBI reports, as unreliable as they are, they clearly show that the latest undisputed recorded time that Maria was last seen was about 6:10-6:15 P.M. Did you hear that? And because of that, even if per chance he did make that phone call, there was ample time according to the old reports for him to do so. The supposed "new evidence" reported throughout the nation as true was in fact not true.

The phrases: "I do not recall." "I don't know." "Approximately" "About" "Sometime after." "At an undetermined time." "I am not certain." That is what is being presented as fact. But I have found that there has been no hint of truth, not the slightest, in what has been presented as fact to the court, and certainly, and just as important, the truth has not been revealed to the public.

It has been stated that the heart of the plea of not guilty by reason of innocence was based upon time frames. The two specific times are the phone call made at about 6:57 P.M. and Tessier's (Cherry's) appearance with recruiters at about 7:15-7:00 P.M. Both supposedly occurred on December 3rd. But the fact is there is no conclusive proof that Jack McCullough made that phone call. Also there is absolutely no proof whatsoever that he was even in Rockford on the night of December 3rd. The only recorded reference to his being there was a record of what he (John Tessier Cherry) had told someone, who told someone else, that he had been in Rockford. Information which was never verified.

The location of where that phone call was made has been presented as new evidence, a claim which has been said is at the heart of the petition to overturn the verdict. This information which has been submitted is that in 1964 the number from which that call was made was at the downtown post office. Prior to that the location is unknown. This is the same information that was discovered during the investigation for the trial. But now the assumption has been made that since that was true in 1964 in was also true in 1957. But here is a factual example of how flawed that assumption is: My home phone number in 1957 was at 616 Archie Place. In 1964 that phone number was across town at 266 Charles Street. Now, I am certain there was a phone at 266 Charles Street in 1957, but it was not the same phone number. Again, the heart of the motion is not factual, and it certainly is not new evidence.

Jack McCullough was quoted as saying, "All I want is for the truth to be told." And when I repeatedly asked why the false claims being made in Jack McCullough's behalf were not being disputed, I was told it was not the time. When I requested to be allowed to argue against the assumptions being represented in court as true, I was told, "There is a time and a place for everything. This is the place but not the time. You will be allowed to speak at the given time." I guess today, after Jack McCullough has been released from prison, is the time.

Jesus said, "In this world you will have trouble. But take heart! I have overcome the world." Heaven knows that we have seen trouble. This has been a horrible ordeal. But I do take heart. And now I pray that God will enable my sister and me, to enable all of us, to grasp, and to hold on to these words of Jesus.

Today, here I am, fifty-nine years after my sister Maria was kidnapped and murdered, four years after Jack McCullough was found guilty beyond any reasonable doubt of her murder, and the story continues to unfold. The darkness tries to seep in. The Devil tries to blacken my heart. But at times like this, times like this that you too will face, I want you to know that God will overcome the darkness just as he has in the past. All I need to do, all that you need to focus on, is the love and eternal presence of God and know with certainty that he changes things.

But take heart!
John 16:33

Prayer: Lord, protect my heart.

O God Eternal, it has been a most difficult time, there are victims everywhere. And yet I find your favors. I thank you, O God Eternal, that you spared my parents from this most difficult of times. I thank you, O God Eternal, as you have strengthened my faith and my trust in you beyond that which I could ever have hoped for. In this I rejoice, even in the midst of times where there has been no rejoicing, and yet, you give me relief.

O God Eternal, continue to protect my heart; continue to shield me. I pray that you enable me to trust that you will give me all that I need to work through this difficult time. I pray that you enable me to face this painful moment, and to know that even it has its important and rightful place. O God Eternal, protect my heart. Give me the strength as my faith is on display to be evidence of your victory which is mine in Christ Jesus. Amen.

In the beginning, unlike my sister Pat, I could not pray for Jack McCullough, the man who was convicted of so brutally murdering my sister. I tried and I could not. I just couldn't, and it troubled me.

On month after the arrest of Jack McCullough for the murder of my sister, I attended my annual Concordia College reunion weekend. This is an entire weekend in which about twenty of my old classmates gather to relive old memories and to accumulate some new ones. And, as we grow older, it is also a time to compare our growing aches and pains. Obviously, at this 2011 reunion, my old friends were interested and concerned with what was going on in my life. As I was sharing with them how difficult and painful this all was, I mentioned that I just could not pray for my sister's killer. I am not sure why or how this came up, but today, as I think about it, I can see that I brought this up because I needed to talk about it. I can see that God prompted this conversation.

My good friend Paul Koester said, "You don't need to pray for him." Paul Koester is the pastor that delivered the sermon at my sister's reburial, and he is a person that is known for thinking before speaking. In fact, many times when you ask him something there is such a long pause before his answer that you wonder if he had heard your question. He said, "You do not need to pray for him." He said you have enough to deal with right now. He said trust in God to do the delivering in his time and in his way.

My sister Pat was able to pray for him. I was not ready. In fact, it is only now, nearly five years later, that I can and do pray for him. And even now it is difficult and the prayers are brief and general. I think the turning point came on Sunday, September 16, 2012, as I was driving to Hampshire, Illinois for worship. The trial was over and we were waiting for sentencing. On that particular Sunday I preached on the question "Are only a few going to be saved." I preached that Jesus had opened the door to heaven for all believers. I shared with the congregation that as I was driving to church the thought came to me that as evil as Johnny was, if he repented and come to faith, that one day he would be in heaven embracing my mother and father along with Maria in the presence of God. That is how complete and powerful the love of God in Christ Jesus is.

Yes. All of a sudden it dawned on me that if Jack McCullough were to come to believe in Jesus Christ as his Lord and Savior, that when he died he would be welcomed into heaven. Not only would he be welcomed into heaven, but he would be greeted with perfect love. He would share in a perfect love which is hard for us to imagine. He would be held in perfect love by all those who have gone before him in Christ Jesus, including my father, my mother, my sister Kay, and most important of all my sister Maria.

This realization, as difficult as it is for me as a hurt and grieving victim, is all important. If we put limits on who God will save, then where does that leave us? If God can and does love and forgive the most vile of sinners, then I must strive to do so as well. But don't beat yourself up over this. Remember now, Christ does not condone the sin. He cannot tolerate evil, and he cannot welcome it into his presence. But he welcomes you and me along with all the repentant and believing Jacks of this world. He welcomes us as perfect and holy children of God shielded and robed in the precious blood and righteousness of Christ Jesus.

Today, I can barely pray for Jack, and I am relieved to know that I do not have to. But, with that being said, I praise and thank God that his great mercy extends to all who come to him in his beloved Son Christ Jesus. I can, I should, and I do pray for his eternal soul. And as I do I am detached from the person, from any evil which he might have committed. As I pray for him I do not see him as he was, as he is, or for what he has done. I pray for him as a lost and condemned sinner. But there are consequences which include temporal or corporal punishment which all of us should be subjected to in this life for the evil we have done. I do not pray for relief from just punishment here on earth, but I pray for his salvation. I pray that the Lord will enable me to love him, just as Jesus loves me, both of which, left to our own, are lost and condemned sinners.

I will punish you as your deeds deserve, declared the Lord.
Jeremiah 21:14

Jesus said, "Neither do I condemn you. Go
now and leave your life of sin."
John 8:11

Prayer: There are no limits to God's Love.

O Gracious God, I thank and praise you for the fact that your love for me, and for all sinners, is complete and powerful. And yet, Lord, the Devil often temps me with thoughts of seeking retribution and punishment against those that have done wrong. I often forget that all have sinned and fall short of the glory of God. I often forget that Jesus came to save sinners, all sinners. Forgive me, O Gracious God.

O Gracious God, I thank you for placing people in my life to council me; to show me the vastness of your mercy. I thank you, O Gracious God, for reminding me over and over again that you will deliver me in your time and in your way. I thank you, Lord, that there are no limits to your forgiveness and your great love in Christ Jesus. And now I pray that you enable me to grow in my ability to forgive as you have forgiven me. Amen.

The horrible notification that someone I had known, a neighbor, had murdered my sister, the arrest, and the unfolding of the story; the trial, the conviction, and the life sentence, all of this was over. I was glad. I was relieved. I was worn out. There was and there is so much talk about closure. It is a nice word, but I must tell you that it is not real. This part of the story had ended, but not the story. Things had changed, and thank God that I now, at least for the most part, view it all differently. That is part of the healing. Going over the events in my mind still bring me pain, but the focus now is different. It is like the death of any loved one. You never stop thinking about them, but the thinking changes. Any major event in your life never leaves you. It is part of you; part of who you are. A tragic event is just that, a tragic event, but God has a way of protecting us, of bringing to us healing. As I have said before, God changes things.

In October of 2013, I received a letter questioning my conclusion that Jack McCullough was guilty of kidnapping and murdering my sister Maria. I was reluctant to respond, but I did. I wrote, "I probably should not be responding to your message of October 12th, however, I do believe that you are sincere in your belief that Jack is innocent of my sister's murder, and that you do deserve a response. I believe that in your mind you're are convinced that Jack is innocent, and I do sympathize with the pain that this brings to you and your loved ones. This trial has been painful for all who are close to it, and the verdict of guilty, even though in our minds it was the correct verdict, is not viewed by the Ridulph family as any sort of victory or any reason to celebrate. But I do believe some good has come from it. It gives hope to so many others, others who may be looking for justice, that it is still possible regardless of how old a case may be. I wish I had some words of comfort to offer you. I will pray for you and your family."

I do not know the reason behind the letter, but this I do know; in responding to the letter I was able to see beyond my pain. I was able to feel his and his family's pain, for they were victims too. They too needed healing. Yes. Evil touches, it burns, all those within its reach.

A stranger from the Southeast wrote to me expressing her sorrow over the pain which we were forced to experience once again. She was able to sympathize with me since she too had been plagued for over twenty-eight years with a tragedy. A tragedy which brought grief and shame to her family. A tragedy which even after so many years, when mentioned would bring her to tears, and unlocked old feelings which she had never been able to come to terms with. She then wanted me to know that I was in her prayers.

Another stranger from the Northeast wrote to me to share her sympathy and to let me know that I was in her prayers.

An old friend wrote to me saying how he and the entire community of Sycamore felt the loss of Maria. He told me he would never forget that December day and how it had changed the face of Sycamore forever.

An old classmate from Concordia wrote to me sharing his sorrow over the nightmare we were going through.

Another old classmate now living in Texas wanted to let me know that her thoughts and prayers have always been with me and my family. She shared with me how that December night in 1957 had rocked our little world. She shared with me that to her Sycamore was never the same. She said that Maria will always be a part of all of us that went through that dreadful night. She wished God's blessing upon us.

A classmate of mine who lived in the neighborhood at the time of Maria's kidnapping wrote to let me know that since the case was re-opened she had been praying for me and my family. She was shocked at how strong of an emotional response she had when she heard about it. She said that what happened to precious Maria back in the 50's was one of those life changing moments. It was a wake-up call to the reality of evil in the world. She then shared her faith in knowing that our reality is reunion, and that one day I will be with my sister forever.

Yes, evil touches everything in its path, but it does not conquer. God changes things. God brings love to light. God delivers us from evil. God provides healing!

You, O Sovereign Lord...out of the goodness of your love, deliver me.
Psalm 109:21

Prayer: God change me, heal me; deliver me.

Heavenly Father, I thank you for changing things. I was lost but now I am found. I was blind but now I see. I thank you. Heavenly Father, tragedy strikes, and tragedy is just that; it is tragic. But you change things. You have a way of protecting and of healing.

Heavenly Father, evil touches; it burns all those within its reach, but, by the grace of God, we make it through the torment. Evil touches everything in its path but it does not conquer. I thank you, Heavenly Father. I thank you for changing things, including me. I thank you for bringing love into the light. I thank you for delivering me from evil. I thank you for providing your healing power. Heavenly Father, I pray that you continue to enable me to see beyond my pain; enable me to see and to feel the pain of others. Heavenly Father, I pray that you continue to change me. I pray for your continued healing. I pray that you deliver me from evil. In Jesus Name. Amen.

It has been said, and I believe it to be true that you have to grieve before you can heal. On Wednesday, April 30, 1958, my sister Maria's earthly remains were laid to rest. That night my sister Kay wrote in her diary, "Chuck didn't cry at all. I was really proud of him."

I don't remember a great deal about that funeral. I remember vividly being there. I remember being surrounded by all the people, especially all of our family and loved ones gathered together from near and from far. I can still see myself there. But it was like a dream, and I don't mean just now, but even then it seemed as though I was dreaming. The one thing I do remember though, so very clearly I remember that I did not cry. I did not cry, and for years that has troubled me. I did not cry.

Whenever we lose a loved one we grieve and we mourn their loss. My father died rather quickly from cancer. He was very active, as a matter of fact he was rototilling his garden when he felt his first pain and thought he had pulled a muscle. He went to the doctor and was diagnosed with advanced cancer and we were told that he had approximately eight weeks to live. He died eight weeks later. During those eight weeks I visited him daily. We would always have a devotion, and we would pray. When he died I grieved, and I still miss him. But the grief was quickly replaced with the joy of knowing with certainty that he was in heaven.

When my mother died a few years later it was a little different. My mother had not been well for a number of years and she was really ready to leave this life and be with her Lord. For several years she would say, "I just don't know why God doesn't take me." And for years I would pray, "Dear Lord, when the time is right, please gently take her home." And, he did. My prayer was answered. And yet, I grieved. And I still miss her. But here again my grief was quickly replaced with joy.

It was different with Maria. Even though I had the same certainty that she was now with her Lord, I had not been able to get past the horror of her death. I had not allowed myself to grieve. How could I heal if I had not grieved? Maria was never far from my thoughts. Maria was often brought up in conversation, even with strangers. I was often asked if it was hard for me to talk about what had happened to her, and I would always respond no. But it was. I had not grieved. I did not cry.

When I was told that Maria's body was going to be exhumed I cried. At the time I never realized the full impact of that. The authorities asked, "When we are finished, just let us know what your wishes are for the reinternment." We were at a loss. Do we just have her re-buried? Do we have a service, a second funeral? If we do should it be private? If private, how private? If we do have a service, what type of service? We asked for advice and were not able to get any because this was something out of the realm of ordinary.

As my sister Pat and I talked about this, she was somehow aware of something I was not. She said, "I have already grieved Maria's death once, but you have not." I did not really get it then, but soon I knew it was true. It was certainly true for me, and it had to a certain respect also be true for her.

We decided on a service, a Christian re-burial service at the church with a committal service at the cemetery. It would be a private service which would include family, intimate friends, most of whom had lived through this tragedy with us from the very beginning. And now, one of the worst things that had ever happened to me, the exhumation of Maria's body, God would use as an instrument of healing as Pat and I began making arrangements for her re-burial.

Stop and consider God's wonders.
Job 37:14

You turn things upside down…
And out of gloom and darkness the eyes of the blind will see.
Isaiah 29:16-18

Prayer: Turn my darkness into something good.

Lord God, Creator of all things, you said let there be light, and there was light. You saw that the light was good, and you separated the light from the darkness. Lord God, you turn things upside down. Let me stop now and consider your wonders.

Lord God, Creator of all things, you have shown me your great victory over sin, death, and the Devil. Let me stop now and consider the victory.

I thank you, Lord, for bringing me to the point where I could grieve Maria's tragic death. I had to grieve before I could heal. Lord, I just could not get past the horror of her death. Lord God, I had not allowed myself to grieve. But you are the Creator of all things good, and I thank you Lord for using my pain for that which is good. I thank you Lord for bringing me out of the gloom and darkness of this tragedy and pain, into the victory over death won by Jesus at the Cross and the Empty Tomb. I pray now, Lord God, that you continue to heal me. I pray that you enable me to stop, consider, and rejoice in your wonders. In Jesus Name. Amen.

The words which I am about to use here are harsh. They pain me deeply. When Maria was kidnapped I did not, I could not, imagine how she was abused. When her half-naked body was found it was lying crumpled up under a fallen tree, exposed to the wintery weather and to hungry animals. My sister Pat summed it up as she said, "She had been discarded like a piece of garbage." As I write these words I become sick to my stomach. And when they exhumed her body we were told that she had been buried in the body bag in which she had been carried out of that desolate woods. Pat said, "This time Maria is going to buried in a dress!" And she was.

The service for the Christian reburial of Maria was held on Sunday, July 22, 2012. The service began at the Evangelical Lutheran Church of St. John at 2:00 in the afternoon and continued with the committal at the Elmwood Cemetery in Sycamore. It was followed by a family gathering and fellowship meal at the Church.

That evening I wrote in my journal: Maria's re-burial was today with family and friends all there. It was so healing. What a blessing that Paul preached. I missed Ken and Chad who could not be there. Oh how God works to mend our broken hearts!"

He heals the brokenhearted and binds up their wounds.
Psalm 147:3

Prayer: Thanks for using those close to us to bring us healing.

Father in heaven, you give me all that I need and so much more. But sometimes I forget. Father, sometimes what comes my way is so horrible that it overpowers me. Father, sometimes I just cannot seem to get out of that desolate woods. It is then my dear Father in heaven, that I see your intervention, and I thank you. Father in heaven, you have put in my life family and friends as your instruments in bringing comfort and healing. And I thank you. You have indeed healed my broken heart, and you bind up my wounds.

Father in heaven, now I pray that when I drift back to that desolate woods that you continue to lead me out; heal my broken heart, and bind up my wounds. Amen.

The service was officiated by Reverend Robert Weinhold from St. John Lutheran Church in Sycamore, Illinois. The message of comfort was delivered by Reverend Paul Koester from Greenfield Park Lutheran

Church in West Allis, Wisconsin. Pastor Koester is a long-time friend and former classmate of mine. It was very important to me to have Paul there, and I am so thankful that my sister agreed with my request. She agreed to have him deliver the message even though she had not met him prior to the service.

The small white fabric covered casket, a replica of her original casket, was carried by four of Maria's nephews; Larry Hickey; Lynn Hickey; Lee Hickey; and Mike Quinn.

The Hymn "Jesus Loves Me", which was sung at Maria's original funeral at the request of my mother, was sung by her great niece Rebekah McFarland. The accompaniment was composed and played by her sister Hannah. This hymn, and these girls, had, and continues to have, such a great impact upon me. I am ever so thankful.

Maria's original casket in 1958 was covered with a spray of pink and white carnations and pink sweetheart roses. A picture of Maria was on the casket among the flowers. On that Sunday of her re-burial, Maria's small coffin covered in plush white fabric was covered with a spray of floral color dominated by pink surrounding that same picture. Next to the coffin stood a large floral cross along with another picture of Maria. When I saw that little casket; as I still see that little casket, my stomach churns. It was so tiny; a harsh reminder of how little she was. A harsh reminder of how she had been taken away so early.

Maria was the first to be buried on April 30, 1958, in what has now become the family plot. Now, 54 years later, she who had preceded them in death, now rejoins her father Michael, mother Frances, sister Kay, and brother-in-law Larry, where together their earthly remains await the coming of our Lord. In 1958 Maria was one of the first to be buried in what was then a new section of the Elmwood Cemetery.

At Maria's original funeral the Reverend Louis Going told those attending that they could find peace in knowing that Maria has reached her everlasting peace. He said, "We can be glad. We can have joy in the midst of this sorrow…if we know the gospel, if we know Christ." Reverend Going said, "She has found herself in the arms of her Lord and

Savior." And then, 54 years later, at a Sunday service, the Reverend Paul Koester stressed that our Lord never forsakes us. Pastor Koester offered the comforting words that Maria was never abandoned; her Savior was always with her. He echoed the words spoken 54 years before that Maria found herself in the arms of her Lord.

At that funeral in April of 1958, Reverend Going read from Maria's obituary that she was baptized on June 11, 1950, and was the proud possessor of three years of perfect attendance in Sunday school. At our gathering after the re-burial service I gave that Sunday school pin to my daughter Maria as a keepsake in memory of her aunt Maria. My daughter Maria, who turned forty-six only the week before, had never been given the opportunity of knowing her name-sake.

As my sister Pat, along with her daughter and granddaughters were putting together a photo array of Maria's life, the girls commented on how painfully visible it was that her life, the life of a little girl, had been so tragically cut short. The Reverend Going, 54 years ago, expressed at Maria's funeral the hope and the prayer that the criminal responsible for her death would be apprehended and dealt with by the courts. And now, after all those years, healing, at least for me had begun. When Rebekah sang "Jesus Loves Me", I cried. And when Paul so appropriately reminded me that Maria was never alone, never abandoned, that her Savior Jesus was always with her, I found such great comfort!

The re-burial service of my sister Maria was on July 22, 2012. It brought me such great comfort! Rebekah singing *Jesus Loves Me*. The certainty of the promise that Jesus never leaves us or forsakes us! Such healing. Such comfort. And then, Good Friday, March 25, 2016, I find myself again being led to that desolate woods. Again old wounds; new anger. Again I must be led to the loving arms of Jesus. Again I must receive his healing power, and comforting words of the certainty that the victory has been won.

I will be with you; I will never leave you nor forsake you.
Joshua 1:14

Prayer: Lord help me know your presence.

Gracious Lord God, how great Thou art! You have promised to never leave us nor forsake us, and I have seen that to be true. I know that to be true. But sometimes, often times, I still let this world and my sinful flesh cloud my vision. Forgive me, Gracious Lord.

Lord, as I am often drawn to that desolate woods, I pray that your Word would ring out loudly in my ear. I know that you did not forsake or abandon Maria, now let me rejoice in knowing that she has reached her everlasting peace. Let me be glad in the Gospel. Heal my wounds. Calm my anger. Let me rejoice. In Jesus Name, and in his victory. Amen.

Maria's tiny re-burial casket was a replica of the original.

Maria's grave after her re-burial.

The exhumation of my sister's body proved to be of little help in the prosecution's case against Jack McCullough, and it caused us so much pain. But I have to once again marvel at how God works.

As my sister Pat and I went through the process of arranging for Maria's re-burial we grew closer. We grieved together, and we healed together. All of the details helped with the healing. We planned the service along with Pastor Weinhold. We selected the participants. We helped with the planning of the luncheon to follow the service. We worked with the florist in selecting the flower arrangements, especially the large floral cross which would remain at the cemetery, a physical sign that Maria had died in the Lord. This was important to us since we were well aware that many would be visiting Maria's grave; many who needed to see this Christian symbol. All of this contributed to my healing. The preparation, the service, the crying, and yes, even the laughter, I needed it all. I needed to grieve, and I needed to heal.

This morning, March 1, 2016, as I am coming down the stairs to begin my day, my wife says, "McCullough is on the front page of the paper again." For me that is not a good way to start any day. I was already a little on edge since McCullough had a new court hearing scheduled for the end of March and the state's attorney was to have prepared a response to his recent petition for the judge's review. This report was due on February 29th and I had requested a copy from his office upon its completion. I had not received it and I was getting a little anxious. I was, to say the least, disappointed to have to read about it first in the newspaper, especially since it appeared that the state's attorney's actions were in direct opposition to the judge's prior instructions. The state's attorney was acting as the defense attorney, and this was very troubling. My first reaction was anger. I felt sick to my stomach. What was I going to do?

Well, first of all I prayed. Secondly I was thankful that I was where I am in the writing of this book. Instead of lashing out directly to the state's attorney, or even indirectly through the press, I have turned to this writing about the process of healing. And as I continue, I have come to the unpleasant realization that the healing of wounds such as this is a process. The healing of wounds such as this will never be complete in this life, but it does, and it has gotten better. There will always be that flare-up, that reminder, that article on the front page in the paper, but now the sting will be slight and brief. Our reactions will be different. You see, the Lord does bring about healing.

My sister Pat called asking about the latest article in the paper. She wondered what it all meant. She wanted to know what I thought. I told her that I was not surprised but that it did upset me. She said she was worried. She was afraid of what Schmack was doing and that she wondered if the judge would see beyond and come to his own right conclusions.

I told Pat that I was not going to call Schmack or again request a copy of his brief so that I could go over the details of it. I said, "I have been given some peace. God has enabled me to heal, and it just would not be healthy for me to dig into this any further." I said, "Why would I chose to re-open those old wounds?" She understood, and she agreed. I told her that we just needed to trust the judge's good judgement. I told her that I would not be surprised if he were to give Schmack a slap on the wrist for not listening to his prior instructions. It seemed clear that the state's attorney was going in a direction other than that which he had been instructed to follow. I needed to thank God for bringing me to the place where I am and to trust that he will continue in his healing.

I am the Lord who heals you.
Exodus 15:26

Prayer: Lord let me respond to your healing.

O God of Comfort, I, we, needed to heal, and in your great love you gave us the means. I needed to cry. I needed to laugh. I needed it all. O God of Comfort, I thank you. And yet we often get anxious. I was troubled. I was angry. I felt lost, and confused. Forgive me O God of Comfort.

You have shown me that the healing which I need is a process. I have seen that there will always be that flare-up, and that reminder. But I thank you for your healing, for now the sting, and now our reactions are different. Yes. I thank you, O God of Comfort, for you do bring about healing.

O God of Comfort, I now pray that you continue your process of healing. I pray that you enable me from re-opening old wounds. I pray that you make me new again. In Christ Jesus. Amen.

For me a large part of the healing was in the sharing. I needed to share. I needed to talk about the tragedy. Was it painful? Yes. But as I shared my pain, as others hurt along with me, it brought me comfort. Not that I wanted anyone else to suffer this loss as I did, but this was something that needed to be shared. And because of the notoriety of our case, the oldest cold case in American history to be tried, our opportunities to share came in other than normal ways, ways other than sharing with our family and friends.

The CBS television network show "48 Hours" received our full support in featuring our case on their program. After the program aired I had this to say: "I would like to say that we were looking forward to seeing how "48 Hours" depicted the events as they unfolded from the beginning of that dreadful night of December 3, 1957, to the judge's pronouncement of life in prison for Jack McCullough. My hope was that the program would put an end to any question of his guilt by a complete and truthful showing of the facts of the case. I hoped for a review of facts which were not brought out at trial since McCullough chose not to present any defense, especially the alibi defense which has been brandished about in the press. I also hoped that this program would bring hope to the many other families who continue to look for answers and for justice for loved ones lost but not forgotten." I went on to say, "My sister Pat and I were very disappointed in the program."

Although we were disappointed in the program, I cannot say that I am sorry that we supported the project. You see, I also had this to say when I was asked about my feelings concerning the show: "The '48 Hours' people have treated us very well from the beginning. They never pressured us for anything, but at the same time they have always been there, almost like another friend leading us along a difficult path. It has been helpful, sometimes painful, and yet sometimes comforting, to be a part of putting this story together. I am hopeful that this program will be another aid in the healing process for myself, my family, and for our community."

Before the show on "48 Hours" was even ready for airing, my sister and I agreed to another project. We would support Charles Lachman in the writing of *Footsteps in the Snow*, a book based upon our case. Charles Lachman was an accomplished author and also the executive producer of the television news magazine show *Inside Edition*. This book led to our appearing on the "Dr. Phil Show", and then a Lifetime Movie Network documentary both based upon the book. At the top of the page in my journal it said, "Every act of trust makes the next act less difficult." On November 3, 2012, I wrote: "As I think over the past year I realize how true it is that acts of trust…seeing the results, makes the next act less difficult! Today Pat, Bill, and I met with Charles Lachman, the executive director of *Inside Edition* and author who wishes to write a book about Maria. It was a good meeting lasting all day. For me it was part of the healing process to talk openly about it."

In response to a Dekalb Chronicle Newspaper reporter's request for comment, I had this to say: "The book *Footsteps in the Snow* and the LMN documentary based upon the book have finally brought to me a sense of conclusion. I feel at ease and at rest, and I am thankful for that. The process has been horribly painful and yet at the same time healing. I now feel able to move on and focus only on the good and pleasant memories. The Bible says, "We know that in all things God works for the good of those who love him." And I believe that to be true. I speak for the Ridulph family in offering our gratitude to all who have been so kind and supportive to us during this difficult time in our lives. The people of Sycamore and the surrounding communities have displayed what it means to truly be a good neighbor and even so much more."

In November of 2014 I wrote, "I now feel able to move on and focus only on the good and pleasant memories." In March and April of 2016, that focus has been threatened. The state had reopened the case, along with it the wounds. The sense of restfulness has been replaced by sleepless nights. I want to, I need to, return to that sense of ease. I need to continue to heal.

Yes, it is time to move on and focus on the good and pleasant memories.

A cheerful heart is good medicine,
But a crushed spirit dries up the bones.
Proverbs 17:22

Prayer: Fill me with good thoughts
and memories so I may heal.

O God of Peace and Joy, you have led me to share my pain. You have placed those in my life to lead me along a difficult path. You have given me the good medicine of a cheerful heart. You have led me away from my crushed spirt that dries up my bones. This process has been painful, but at the same time healing. I thank you. You have given me rest, and I thank you. You have enabled me to move on and to focus on the good and pleasant memories, and I thank you.

O God of Peace and Joy, I now pray that you enable me to continue on that path which is good. I pray that you continue to guard my heart. I pray for your continued good medicine. In Christ Jesus. Amen.

And I was moving on. In my journal for December 2, 2012, the theme was "God is good and his mercy endures forever", and I wrote: "I preached at Trinity this morning and then delivered a Christmas message at the annual candlelight service at Oak Crest. What a blessing! Tomorrow will be fifty-five years since Maria was kidnapped and the next day will be 25 years since I had a drink."

I was moving on. In my journal, on Christmas night 2012, I wrote: "Even though I have not always done what is right in God's sight yet he has still richly blessed me. We were all together today for Christmas! This is the first Christmas I have spent with Maria in over forty years. This, as my sister Pat would say, is indeed a God thing. I could not be more thankful!"

I was moving on. On New Year's night 2013, I wrote in my journal: "Maria invited us all to her house. It was a great surprise! We all went, including Betty (Maria's mother) and her husband Steve. All went well but being around Betty makes it a painful reminder of all those lost years with Maria. I need to pray about that but boy do I praise God for the chance to be with Maria now!"

Yes. I was moving on.

Chapter Six

The Remembering

Last night my wife told me that she had heard my old house on Archie Place was soon going up for sale and that when it did she would like to go through it. It is at moments like this that I recognize how I have healed over the years. There was a time, a time not in the too distant past, when thinking about our old house would have been painful. But that was not the case last night. Last night the reminder of my old home brought with it a rush of good memories, and I too am looking forward to going through my old home if and when they have an open house.

I have so many good memories of growing up as a child. How awful it would be to have them repressed or overpowered by evil. And the same is now true when I think of my sister Maria. Yes, when I think of her there are always thoughts of that horrible night which so tragically impacted my life. But I thank God that he has allowed me to see beyond that.

That first day in court, when I was called to the witness stand at the trial of Jack McCullough for the kidnapping and murder of my sister, I was asked to describe her. Although I knew I was going to be asked that question, it was still difficult to get the words out. I said, "She was a very smart girl, a gifted child. She liked to sing. She liked to read. She was a very active child, friendly, outgoing, athletic. I often described her as a tomboy, but as I think about it, she really didn't do tomboy things. She spent her time on girl things, playing with dolls, having tea parties and things that girls do. She was a very pretty young girl. She was tall, slender, dark haired, and always seemed to be smiling." But how sad that it was so hard at the time picturing my precious little sister because of the circumstances. I was describing a little girl that had been so brutalized it was beyond imagination, and it hurt so deeply. But today as I write those same words it is different. Today I see beyond that. Today I see the beautiful little girl that she was.

When I think of my old house on Archie Place I think of laughter. I think of family. I think of mom reading to Maria before bed. I think of Pat playing the piano. I think of Kay practicing her voice lessons. I think of eating dinner together. I think of Maria playing in her corner with her dolls. I think of eating baked apples from Maria's Easy Bake Oven, a hand-me-down from her sister Kay. And, when not too long ago, at a church dinner when we had baked apples for desert, I was able to share with those around me that the last time I had baked apples it was with my sister Maria. And I was able to share that wonderful memory with a smile.

On July 31, 2013, my granddaughter McKenzie and I drove up to Madison, Wisconsin to watch my daughter Maria's step-son Chase play Ultimate Frisbee. I really was not familiar with the sport but McKenzie is up for anything sports related, especially something new, and I of course jumped at the chance to spend some time with Maria and her family.

My son-in-law Joe prepared a great picnic lunch featuring his out of this world home-made chicken salad, and God provided a beautiful late summer afternoon and evening. The game was fun to watch even though Chase's team lost. But what really stuck out in my mind was watching my grandson Elliot and granddaughter Phoebe rolling around playfully in the grass. Elliot was eleven, about to be twelve, and Phoebe was three, going on four. You would have thought that Phoebe would have had no chance, but she was fearless and unrelenting. My granddaughter McKenzie, who is fearless herself, said to me, "Boy, is Phoebe going to be tuff!" There they were laughing and screaming with the laughter and screams all blended into one.

I have not been able to get this picture out of my mind, this picture of an older brother roughhousing with his little sister. It is something like nothing else. No one else can experience it. Not two brothers. Not two sisters. Not an older sister and a younger brother. No one else.

I can't get it out of my mind, and this picture brings back the memories of my own roughhousing with my little sister Maria. I can still hear the same laughter and the same screams. I can recall my mother's shouts from the other room, or through the window into the back yard, "Chuck, stop making Maria scream!" Yes, there is nothing like an older brother roughhousing with his little sister.

When I was discussing the time frames and different scenarios of what might have happened in that alley way on that December 3rd evening of 1957 with Larry Kot of the Illinois State Police, I shared with him how Maria would never have gone willingly. I shared with him how Maria would have fought and screamed. It is no wonder that Johnny Tessier (Jack McCullough) was reported to have been seen with multiple scratches by the recruiters in Rockford. But oh how it sickens me to think that the last sounds to come from her lips would be screams of fear instead of the laughing and screams of joyful and loving play between an older brother and his little sister.

And so I try not to think of that dreadful moment. Instead I smile as I think of that picture of my grandchildren Elliot and Phoebe rolling around in the grass laughing and screaming. I smile as I remember so vividly those childhood days of roughhousing with my sister Maria.

I have often talked about what Maria might have been had she been allowed to grow up. I think about Maria all the time, and I remember her perfectly. But today was the first time that I ever thought about, this is the first time that I ever said, "Boy! Would we have been good friends!" My wife Diane was in bed sick. I was just sitting at home and thinking it would have been nice to have been able to go visit mom or dad, as I often do, and it hit me. Maria and I would have been good friends.

Hate what is evil; cling to what is good.
Romans 12:9

Prayer: Help me cling to what is good.

O God of Joy, you have over and over again told me about the joy which you want me to have. You Word is filled with promises of joy. And I cling to that. But Lord, I must admit that it is much easier when things are going well. When I am challenged and confronted with tragedy and pain, I often falter. O God of Joy, I need your continued and ever-present help.

I praise you for allowing me to see beyond the tragedy, beyond the pain. What happened to Maria hurts so deeply. The thought of her last moments sickens me. But today I see beyond that. Today I see the beautiful little girl that she was. Today I am able to share loving memories with a smile. Today I think of the good memories. And I thank you. I praise you. And I continue to pray that you allow me to cling to that which is good. Amen.

Konnie, a close friend of my sister Kay's was often at our house on Archie Place. At that time in 1957 she lived in our neighborhood. In September of 2012 she wrote, "I talked with Kay about a week before she died. We laughed and we talked a lot about our love for the Lord and our gratitude to him for sustaining us through the pain...The events of December 3, 1957 were burnt on my mind and continue to be as vivid as they have ever been. I have a photo that was taken at one of Kay's birthday parties, of Maria, Kay, and me. I have always cherished that picture and the memory of happier times it brings. It seems to me that everyone who knew Maria loved her. Sometimes friend's little sisters can be pests. That was not so with Maria. I am writing to let you know that you and Pat are both in my prayers as you continue to relive the pain of that awful night and all that you and your family have had to endure. My heart aches for you all."

I too remember Maria always being around. Yes, always there, but never being in the way; never being a pest. It may be hard to believe, but I cannot ever remember her being unhappy. Now that is something. Yes, that is some memory.

Chuck helping Maria with her 1st place Kid's Day parade entry.

I have already mentioned that the process of healing from such a traumatic tragedy is exactly that, a process. And today the remembering is still mixed with the reliving, and the good memories are often a little tainted with some pain. For example, I have just shared with you my overwhelmingly good memories when I see or hear about my childhood home. But at the same time, when I drive by that corner of Archie Place and Center Cross, the place from where Maria was taken from us, as I often do, I cringe. And when I continue one block driving past the Tessier house, I am flooded with emotion. I have even gone so far as to say that I wish that house would be torn down. Is that healthy? No it is not.

I have heard your prayer and seen you tears; I will heal you.
2 Kings 20:5

Prayer: Turn my tears into joy.

Gracious Father, you have created all that is good, and nothing that is bad. I pray that you help me to remember that. You see, my memories are often tainted with that which is bad, and that is not healthy for me, or for those around me. Gracious Father, you have seen my tears, now hear my prayer. Please Father, help me to find joy in the good memories, and to discard the bad.

Gracious Father, you created for me that which is good; now I pray that you enable me to grasp your good and gracious gifts, including my memories, and to cast out the bad. Gracious Father, you have heard my prayer, and seen my tears. Now, let me trust in your healing. In Jesus Name. Amen.

What happened in Sycamore on that December evening in 1957 had an impact on all of the town, and that night has been remembered in so many ways throughout the years. A huge full-color porcelain map of 1958 Sycamore measuring eight feet square hung on the outside front wall of the Municipal building. In Bold letters at the top it read, **IN MEMORY OF MARIA RIDULPH.** This memorial was paid for with money donated for a reward which was being offered for information just after Maria's abduction. It remained there for over forty-five years even though the map had long since been outdated. It was replaced with a pedestal memorial plaque in front of the building.

When the time came (which in reality was long overdue) to take down or replace this memorial map, it was handled with care so as to not upset our family. Mayor Ken Mundy, who is one of my oldest and dearest friends, gave me a call to approach the subject. He said, "The city would like to replace Maria's memorial map because it has become outdated." He went on to make it clear that they wanted to replace it with something more lasting and wondered if I would meet with the city manager to discuss possible options. I was in total agreement and was glad that they had asked me to participate in the project.

It was decided to erect a pedestal in front of the Municipal Building just under the location of the original memorial. I was honored to be asked if I would like to design the bronze plaque. And I did. The new memorial has an engraved picture of Jesus embracing little children with this Bible verse from Mark 9:37 just below it: *Jesus said, "Whoever welcomes one of these little children in my name welcomes me."* The top of the plaque reads as follows:

IN MEMORY OF
Maria Elizabeth Ridulph
March 12, 1950 – December 3, 1957

And the bottom of the plaque reads: *This is in memory of Maria Elizabeth Ridulph who on December 3rd, 1957, was kidnapped while playing near her home. She was found murdered in the spring of 1958. This is also in honor of the great people in our community that reached out with their love and compassion.*

I drive by, or ride my bike by, or walk by this memorial often, and it is a great comfort to me. The city of Sycamore, in kindness and great respect, unknowingly provided such healing for me. This healing came in not only the process of bringing this memorial into being, but also for enabling me and the many others that see this memorial to remember Maria who is now in the loving arms of Jesus her Savior. Just this past week, Monday, April 18, 2016, I was riding my bike on a summer-like spring day. As I often do, I rode through the cemetery and visited Maria's grave. There on her grave was a bouquet of pink flowers placed by some unknown person who had come to love Maria. As I continued to ride through town, I rode past Maria's memorial in front of the Sycamore Police Department. There on the plaque was a bouquet of yellow baby roses.

During the recent commotion and turmoil of court proceedings, proceedings which led to the release of Jack McCullough from prison, I was asked if I felt that Maria was being forgotten in the conflict that was going on. I did not hesitate in my answer. The support and love of the people of Sycamore, Illinois and the surrounding community has never faltered from the very beginning. Maria would never be forgotten.

My sister Pat and I created the Maria Ridulph Memorial Fund, a fund which will be used to benefit young students. The plan is to select students which are or have been students at the West Elementary School in Sycamore, Illinois. West School is where my sister Maria attended. The fund was established in 2015 and the first students to benefit from the fund will be this year, 2016.

Barry Schrader, a local author whose book "Hybrid Corn & Purebred People" was released in 2015, held a book signing event to which I was invited. He had so graciously offered to donate a portion of the sales to the Maria Ridulph Memorial Fund. He also had plans of writing a children's book on the history of DeKalb County Illinois that he was dedicating to the memory of my sister Maria. As part of that project he asked me to write a short description of who Maria was for the children. This is what I wrote:

You would have liked my sister Maria, she was seven years old going on eight when she was taken from us. So many people have asked me what I thought she might have been when she grew up. I have thought about that I guess; but I think more about what she was.

Maria was a bright cheerful child, full of excitement. I was just looking at the picture of her that my mother had taken on her first day of school. No fear there. No. She was fearless, confident, excited about the opportunity of going to school to learn, and of course to play.

You see, Maria was a friendly child; a bit of a "tomboy" and at the same time very "girlish". She loved to run, dance, sing, play with dolls, bake on her easy bake oven, and hold tea parties. She was smart, pretty, good at school, and knew how to make a "firm" snowball. Maria was a lot like you, and I know that you would have loved to have called her your friend.

Maria loved Jesus, and Jesus loved her. So, you see, when I am asked about what she would have been, it is much more important to remember who she was, and to know that she is now in heaven with Jesus.

Maria's first day of school. Notice her confident expression.

Thus far has the Lord helped us.
1 Samuel 7:12

"Thus far has the Lord helped us." These words from the Bible are in reference to a thanksgiving memorial erected to the glory of God and for the encouragement of his children Israel. The setting was a time of a religious meeting of the Israelites. It was a time when they were experiencing trouble from their enemies. It is an example of how sometimes evil seems to come out of good. A reminder that when sinners, when we begin to repent and reform, we must expect that Satan will muster all his force against us. But we are shown how good is ultimately brought out of that evil.

The Israelites were repenting and praying when they were attacked. They were totally unprepared for battle. What did they do? They told Samuel, "Do not stop crying out to the Lord our God for us." And the Lord answered him. In thanks, a memorial to the victory was set up. He named the memorial Ebenezer, meaning *The stone of help.* And he said, "Thus far has the Lord helped us."

Prayer: Lord help me to remember your goodness.

Gracious Lord, God of all Mercies, you have not only revealed your great love to us in Christ Jesus, but you have also provided us with the love and support of those you have placed around us. And yet you have warned us that we must be watchful. We must be watchful for Satan is ever ready to pounce. I have seen the memorial. I have seen the evidence of your help, and I praise you.

Gracious Lord, God of all Mercies, lead me to pray for your continued deliverance. Lead me to see the victory. Lead me to remember your goodness. Amen.

Chapter Seven

The Emotions

This is the chapter which really led me to write this book. All of the emotions which come into play as we are faced with any tragedy in our lives. Many, perhaps even most victims may not even realize how deeply and completely they have been impacted, and yet, at some point all of these emotions must be recognized and dealt with.

We all have emotions, and they are here to stay. What does the Bible say about emotion? Are emotions something that are negative or positive? Does God want me to be happy? How can I control my emotions? What connection is there between feelings and fears? You see, emotions can be our best friend or our worst enemy, and emotions are there and they are given to you by God. You can either lie about them or ignore them, or you can learn to do something with them. For one thing that is certain about emotions, we all have them. But unfortunately there are times when the emotions have us, and it is when the emotions have us that they become a problem.

Well, what are emotions? They are feelings on the inside, which are caused by pain or pleasure, and they will try to move you in a certain direction. Webster's Dictionary has this to say: Emotion is an agitation; strong feeling; any disturbance. Emotion is a departure from the normal calm state of such a nature as to include strong feeling, an impulse toward open action, and certain internal physical reactions. Now that is some strong stuff don't you think? And, if you have negative feelings, they will try to move you away from God's purpose and destiny for your life. If your feelings control you, they will try to move you away from the will of God and away from having a good relationship with Him.

I should not have to say it, but the fact is the Devil will use your emotions against you. He wants to tempt you through your feelings so you are moved away from God and his purpose for you. But the good news is that God also wants to use your emotions to move you towards him. And the emotion he uses is based in love, then peace, and then joy. Yes, he wants to show his love to you, because then you will seek him and start to believe and trust him.

Is it a sin to have negative feelings and emotions? No. But it is what the negative feelings and emotions can lead you to that can become a sin. Jesus also had negative emotions, but he was not ruled by them. And this is how it can be for you as well.

We are created by God to master life, and not that life should control us. There is a reason why God has given us emotions, but they were not intended as something that should have power over us. No. We should be in control over them. You see, God has created us to show compassion and love, but sin, the Devil, and the curse that Adam brought into this world, have in many ways destroyed these emotions so that negative feelings will harm us and others around us.

Now, I want you to know that you do not, you should not, have to believe the Devil's lies when he says to you: "You will never overcome this, you will always be under these feelings, and this is the way you are." I want you to know that God will give you the power to overcome all the negative things that come your way. And having control over your emotions is not to say that you cannot have feelings. For you have that! But I am talking about being able to handle feelings in a right way, so that you are in control of your emotions, not the emotions controlling you.

These are the emotions, or the areas which needed to be addressed in my life over the years: Why; Worry; Fear; Helplessness; Emptiness; Sense of loss; What to do; How to act; Silence; Anger; Guilt, Revenge; Forgiveness; Acceptance; and Being alone. Each of these areas are extensive. For example: Anger at the loved one (victim); at self; at authorities; at family; at killer; at judicial system; at the press; at witnesses; and sometimes even at God. I am going to deal with each but not in any particular order, especially not in any order of importance. These will all affect us differently, but I am certain that they will in fact affect us all. And then I am going to discuss the powerful emotions of love, peace, and joy, which God uses to overcome the negative in our lives.

I have given you authority to overcome all the power
of the enemy; nothing will harm you.
Luke 10:19

Prayer: Dealing with emotions

O Lord, my Guide, and my Protector, you give to your children, to me, only that which is good. However, the Devil often uses your good and gracious gifts to entice me away from your presence. You have given me emotions, and you use these emotions to move me closer and closer to you. But the Devil would use my emotions against me. The Devil wants to tempt me through my feelings away from you and your purpose for me. O Lord, my Guide, and my Protector, it is not sinful to have negative feelings or emotions, but it is what they can lead me to that can become a sin. And I confess, O Lord, that sometimes my emotions get the better of me. I confess, O Lord, that sometimes, often times, my emotions control me. Sometimes they move me in the wrong direction. Sometimes they move me away from your purpose and your destiny for my life. Forgive me.

O Lord, my Guide, and my Protector, I pray that you enable me to recognize the Devil's lies. O Lord, I pray that you enable me to grow in the emotions of love, peace, and joy. I pray that you give me the power to overcome all the negative things that come my way. O Lord, I pray that you enable me to handle my emotions so that they draw me ever closer to you and your guiding and protecting hand. In Jesus Name. Amen.

WORRY: I chose to begin with worry since this is the first emotion that came into play for me, and it is also an emotion which simply does not want to give up. Webster describes worry as to harass with or as if with continual snapping or biting; to shake and mangle with the teeth as "the dog was worrying the rat." To torment; trouble; plague.

When I was a kid we had this dog named Mitzi. She was a springer spaniel and the greatest companion, but primarily a hunting dog. In the summer time she had to be tied up in the back yard because we did not want her wandering through the neighborhood gardens. But in the winter she was allowed to roam. This dog became just another of my playmates, and I would often take her along when out to play. We had this wooded area next to Johnson's Greenhouse where we would play all sorts of stuff, anything from army to hide & seek. I can remember on more than one occasion how Mitzi would corner a possum or some other wild thing in that woods. She would circle, and circle that animal until she got that opportunity to grab it with her teeth by the back of the neck. She would then just shake it, and shake it, until it was dead. As hard as I tried I could not get Mitzi to let go. Not a pretty picture. So when I hear this definition of worry I understand. I can visualize how deadly worry can be.

It was not long after my sister was missing that I began to worry; a little at first, and then it grew and it grew. Worry took over and began to plague me. And it was contagious. It spread first throughout our house, then the neighborhood, the town, and eventually the nation. Yes. The worry grew like the plague.

Jesus said, "Do not worry." (Matthew 6:25) Well, the fact is that too many of us have been trapped in the mind-set of worry and the anxiety of it all is choking us. You see, worry can and will consume you if you are not careful. We all know that don't we? I believe every physician alive will tell you the same thing: Worry will kill you. And yet, what do we do? We worry. It just doesn't make any sense does it?

When Jesus tells us not to worry he is giving us more than just some good advice. He is giving us some life-saving advice. And you know what else? It is more than advice. It is in fact a directive. He says plainly and directly, "Do not worry." And yet, we worry.

In one of my Old Testament courses when I was studying for the ministry I was required to write a paper on a prominent Biblical character. Two of the choices given to us were David, whom I chose, and Abraham. David, described as the one whom God loved, turned out to be someone that I did not like very well. But one thing about David was that even though he often sinned, and sinned greatly, he would quickly repent and turn back to God when he was confronted with his sin. But Abraham, often referred to as the father of our faith, whom I did not chose to write about, I did like. I especially liked, and I often think about, the time when God told him to just pack-up and go. God told him to get going and I will tell you to stop when you get there.

Well, Abraham had it made where he was for God had richly blessed him. But still, he simply packed-up and went just as he had been told. He went without even knowing where he was going. He never questioned it. He simply went because God had told him to go. Now that is faith. That is trust. That is putting aside worry. And as a result God richly blessed him. Abraham was not overwhelmed with worry about what lied ahead. He simply trusted in the Lord, and he went.

But still, if you are anything like me, we worry. Yes, worry continues to nip at the back of my neck. It tries, and it tries to get its death grip upon me. It began with worrying about where my sister was, and has continued to nip at me as today I find myself worrying about what the states' attorney will do next. But I thank God that my trust in him has by far outgrown my struggle with worry.

Martha was distracted...She came to Jesus and asked,
Lord, don't you care...
The Lord answered, "You are worried and upset about many things,
but only one thing is needed. Mary has chosen what is better,
and it will not be taken away from her.
Luke 10:40-41

Martha was distracted, and the Devil will distract us as well. He will use worry to get between us and our Lord. What was it that her sister Mary had chosen? She chose to get as close to Jesus as she possibly could.

God is our refuge and strength, an ever-present help in trouble.
Therefore we will not fear, though the earth give
way, and the mountains fall into the sea,
Though its waters roar and foam and the
mountains quake with their surging.
Psalm 46:1-3

Prayer: Enable me to trust rather than worry.

Eternal Father, I praise you for who you are and for what you have done. You have left no room for any doubt of your great love. You have left no room for any doubt of your great power. You have left no room for any doubt that you can, you have, and you will continue to provide all that I need, and so much more. And yet, I worry. My worries just do not want to give up! I understand, I can visualize, I have experienced, how terrible, deadly even, worry can be. And yet, I worry. Eternal Father, forgive me.

Eternal Father, you have shown me your many, and your great mercies. I thank you for that, for it is the source of my deliverance from worry. And yet, I begin to worry; a little at first, and then it grows and it grows. Eternal Father, forgive me.

Eternal Father, I pray that you would by the power of the Holy Spirit increase my trust in you. Father, I pray that when worry begins to creep into my thinking that you enable me to simply turn to you for the peace of mind, and the peace of heart, which only you can give. Yes. I pray that you deliver me from worries. Amen.

FEAR: Fear and worry seem to go hand-in-hand don't they? One seems to breed the other. Fear is described as a painful emotion marked by alarm. It is associated with panic, terror, and horror, also anxious concern. And for me, on that tragic night of December 3, 1957, it did not take long for my worries to turn into fear. And fear, like worry, continues to be a demon which just wants to attach itself to me.

You know what, if you are anything like me, and I would guess that you are, we can fear just about anything. I fear the worst, and I fear the slightest. The Devil just waits for my guard to be down and in slips worry then fear, or fear then worry. But just as Jesus said, "Do not worry" (Matthew 6:25), so he also said, "Don't be afraid." Jesus said, "Don't be afraid, just believe." Mark 5:36.

When fear starts to creep in, as it often does even throughout each and every day, this is what I do. I say, "The victory has been won!" Yes. I remind myself that God has conquered all in Christ Jesus. I remind myself that I need not fear. Jesus has conquered sin, death, and the Devil. What else is there for me to fear?

Yes. Bad things will continue to happen to me, and bad things will happen to you. But the final victory has been won, and if God is for us, then who can be against us? And yet, just as worry is a constant enemy, so fear seems to be a constant companion. And fear can and often does dictate all that we are and what we do or cannot do. Yes, fear can really take us over, and I don't mean the healthy kind of fear which tells us not to touch a hot stove or run in front of a moving bus. I mean the fear of the unknown, the fear which comes from not trusting in an all-powerful God.

I want you to think about something for a moment. I want you to think about the fears which have confronted you in the past. I want you to think about the fears which have so often made your life miserable, perhaps even unbearable at times. How many of those things which you so terribly feared actually came to pass? I would guess that if you are anything like me, probably very few if any. And you know what else? When you spend all that precious time in fear, you are simply wasting God given opportunities to bask in the rich blessings that he has in store for you. It just doesn't make sense does it? Doesn't it just make a lot more sense to simply trust in your all loving and powerful God?

Still, it is true that many things bring fear into our hearts. But we do not have to give in. Jesus said, "Trust in God. Trust also in me." John 14:1. Yes, the way to get over the paralysis of fear is to turn the situation over to God and then trust him. Yes, you and I will be confronted with fear, but you are not alone. God is with you. And God is in control. Yes, if God is for you, then who can be against you?

I am the Lord, your God, who takes hold of
your right hand and says to you,
"Do not fear; I will help you."
Isaiah 41:13

Fear not...When you pass through the waters, I will be with
you; and when you pass through the rivers, they will not
sweep over you; and when you walk through the fire, you
will not be burned; the flames will not set you ablaze.
Isaiah 43:2

Prayer: Do not fear.

Gracious Father, Caretaker of my soul, and Protector of my life, why am I so often overcome with fear? Why do I worry and then allow my worries to turn to fear? Gracious Father, my Caretaker, and my

Protector, why is my life often plagued with anxious and useless fear? Why can't I just trust you? Forgive me.

Gracious Father, fear is a demon which wants to attach itself to me. The Devil waits for my guard to be down and in slips worry and then fear, or fear and then worry. Gracious Father, you have shown me the victory. Jesus has said, "Do not worry". Jesus has said, "Don't be afraid." But where is my trust? Forgive me.

Gracious Father, you have delivered me over and over again, and I thank you. Yes, bad things will happen, but you have shown me the victory. And I thank you. Now, my Caretaker and my Protector, I pray for the strength to cast off my fears. I pray that your Spirit enable me to feel your hand as you take hold of me and say, "Do not fear. I will help you." I pray that your Spirit enable me to sense, to see, to feel your presence, and to know that the flames will not set me ablaze. In Jesus Name. Amen.

HELPLESSNESS: My sister Maria was gone. We did not know where, how, or why. There were people all around. We were surrounded by family, friends, neighbors, and even strangers; people in authority, and just plain people. And I think that all of them felt just as helpless as we did. All of us wanted to do something. We felt compelled to do something, but did not know what. We cried out in despair, "Oh my God!" Believers and non-believers alike, silently, and perhaps unknowingly, prayed, "Oh my God!" And yet we felt helpless. And as the hours turned into days, even as our prayers became more focused and more intense, we felt even more helpless. If only there was something we could do. If there was only something anyone could do to bring Maria back to us safe and sound.

Fifty-five years later, at Maria's second burial service, Pastor Paul Koester said, "Maria was never alone. Maria was always in the arms of Jesus." WOW! Maria was never alone. We felt helpless and lost but God had heard our prayer. Maria was never alone. Even before we uttered the words, God was holding Maria. Yes. While we were crying out for someone to help, for someone to do something, God was already in action.

Today this brings me great comfort. But at the time, if someone had said those words to me I doubt that I would have heard them. The pain, the fear, was just too great. I was not ready to be helped. I too needed to be held by my Lord. I needed to be nurtured and led out of that helplessness. And you know what? That feeling of helplessness served its purpose. When we are weak, even to the point of helplessness, were do we turn? Naturally, instinctively, we turn to a source of strength. Yes. I can do nothing, but with God all things are possible.

Today I know that there are just certain things which are beyond my control. There are certain things which I do not agree with and even simply find repelling, but cannot change. It is in these circumstances that I must turn them over to God. Is it easy? For me it is difficult. I seem to fight it even when I know that it works. But the more I turn to God for help, the more I heal, and the less helpless I feel.

I lift up my eyes to the hills; where does my help come from?
My help comes from the Lord, the Maker of heaven and earth.
Psalm 121:1

Hills and mountains are majestic in appearance aren't they? At least that is how they were viewed in times of old, and the hills of Jerusalem and the hill on which the temple stood were especially thought of as majestic. They were thought of as places of refuge. "I lift up my eyes to the hills; where does my help come from? My help comes from the Lord, the Maker of heaven and earth." "I life up my eyes."

Today many if not most churches are built with high, I mean really high ceilings, and as you enter the sanctuary your eyes are drawn up above. And as you look up, you are reminded that your help comes from above. Your help, my help, comes from God. Yes, my help comes from the Lord, the Maker of heaven and earth. We need this reminder, and here in the Psalms our Lord paints the perfect picture. We are reminded of where our help comes from. We are reminded of who our Lord is. Yes. He who so majestically created all things remains active in all of his marvelous creation as our all-powerful helper.

But some of you may be saying that is not true. You may be thinking it is not true because of the tragedy which has plagued you. You may be wondering how I can possibly say such a thing after my sister Maria was taken so tragically at such a young age. Yes, just what exactly does it mean that the Lord will keep us from all harm? When tragedy strikes do we sometimes hear, or do we even proclaim, "Where is God now?" But the Bible tells me, in fact the Lord tells me that he will watch over me. All I need to do is lift up my eyes and see Jesus. Yes, as I confront the tragedies from my past, or the turmoil which swirls around me now, or even to any troubles which may come my way in the future, all I need to do is fix my eyes on Jesus. You see, for I am helpless, but my Lord is not.

Prayer: When I feel helpless.

Lord of heaven and earth, Creator of all things, you are the source of the help that I so often need, and I praise you. I felt helpless. Even as I prayed I felt helpless. I felt the need to do something, but did not know what or how. I felt helpless. But you heard my prayer. Even before I uttered the words, you were holding Maria. And today I am comforted by that, but then I was not ready. I too needed to be held by you. I too needed help. I needed to be led out of that helplessness.

Lord of heaven and earth, you lifted my eyes to the hills. You reminded me that my help comes from you. And I thank you. You reminded me that I can do nothing, but with you all things are possible. And I thank you. Trust is what I needed, and trust is what I lacked. But you heard my prayer, and you helped me. And I thank you.

Lord of heaven and earth, now I pray for your continued help. I pray that you lift my eyes always up to you. I pray for your guidance and your strength. I pray for your healing so that the more I heal, the less helpless

I feel. Lord of heaven and earth, I pray all this in confidence, for in your strength I am not helpless. Amen.

EMPTINESS: The reality has set in. My sister was gone, and even before we knew with certainty what had happened, we had begun to believe the worst. Even though we were surrounded with people, loving people, God fearing people, we felt different. Here I wanted to say *alone*, that we felt alone, but it was not that. It was something different. We had been drained. We were near empty. And here again I almost said, *We were empty.* But as I did, this is what came into my mind: *A bruised reed he will not break.* This is from the prophet Isaiah in the Old Testament. *A bruised reed he will not break, and a smoldering wick he will not snuff out. Isaiah 42:3*

When I completed my instruction for prison ministry I was given a lapel pin which depicted a bent reed. It was attached to a card quoting those words from Isaiah. I often wear this pin, and it is a constant reminder to me that no matter how frail we might be, no matter how damaged, God will bind us up so that we can stand straight. God provides the oil so that we can burn brightly again. And so, this tragedy had left us near empty, but not alone.

I was in this fog, like I was alone. I could see what was going on around me, but I was somehow detached. The house was full. People were talking to me. But it did not seem real. I was filled with emotion. I wanted to cry. I wanted to shout. But there was nothing there. Everything was different. The room which I had shared with my little sister instead of being filled with laughter was now filled with an empty bed. Her corner in the living room which she had claimed for herself was there. Her stuff was there. But she was not. Her place at the dinner table was empty, and so it seemed was I.

The feeling of emptiness is beyond description really. The dictionary describes it as containing nothing; vacant, unoccupied, hollow. As I sit here and try to describe how I felt I struggle to find the words. But thank God for this: We will never know total emptiness. *In the beginning God created the heavens and the earth. Now the earth was formless and empty, darkness was over the surface of the deep, and the Spirit of God was hovering over the waters. Genesis 1:1-2.* You see, God was, and God will always be there! And God was there for me when I felt empty; when I was broken.

Today I still miss my sister Maria, and nothing can ever change that until that time when we are re-united in heaven. But that missing is different. Today, right now, when I think about Maria's little corner in the living room on Archie Place, it is not empty. She is there laughing and playing.

This is what the Lord says; he who created the heavens, he is God;
He who fashioned and made the earth, he founded it;
He did not create it to be empty.
Isaiah 45:18

Prayer: We are not empty.

Eternal Lord, Creator of all that is, I praise you. You merely spoke the word, and all that is came into being. I praise you. You have shown your great love and your almighty power, and yet, when tragedy struck, I felt different. I felt drained. I felt emptiness. But then, Eternal Lord, you restored me. I praise you. Yes, Lord, no matter how damaged, no matter how frail I might be, you bind me up so that I might again walk straight. You provide the oil so that I might burn brightly again. I thank you.

Eternal Lord, this tragedy left me near empty, but not alone. I was somehow detached; nothing seemed real. I wanted to cry. I wanted to shout, but there was nothing there. Everything was different. The loss was overwhelming. But, in the midst of this terrible state, one thing remained the same: You were there. Eternal Lord, Creator of all that is, you were there. My life was not empty. You were there, and you brought life and light into the darkness.

Today, Eternal Lord, I thank you that things have changed. Today I pray for your continued presence. I pray that you continue to fill that empty feeling with all the rich blessings which only you can give. I pray that you continue to fill me to the full. In Jesus Name. Amen.

GUILT: I have this old jewelry box. It is falling apart and I am not sure when or from where I ever got it, but in it I keep some of my treasures. The treasures which my wife Diane says will be set out on the curb, thrown out when I die. That is most likely true, but none-the-less, they are treasures to me. In that old box I have this little, tiny actually, wicker basket. It was my sister Maria's. In it I have this tiny picture on an aluminum disc. It is of my daughter Maria along with my daughter Diane when they were very little. It is one of the few pictures that I have of them before my daughter Maria was taken from me.

I found this little basket when after some length of time we had begun to pack-up my sister Maria's things around the house. And this little basket contained some of Maria's treasure. It held a few pennies, a nickel, a dime, and two quarters. I had vowed to keep them forever, but somewhere along the line I spent her treasure. I still have that little basket, and I treasure it, but I sure wish I still had those coins. I have never told this story before. And it hurts me deeply to tell it now. Guilt is a terrible thing.

I looked up guilt in Webster's Dictionary and I found that the definition just does not do it justice. Guilt is horrible. Guilt like worry can destroy. Guilt is one of the most crippling diseases among people today. Psychiatrists and doctors say that unresolved guilt is the number one cause of mental illness and suicide. They tell of how it prompts millions of Americans to gulp down pills to tranquilize their anxiety. Gordon MacDonald, a pastor and author said, "We cannot expect to live healthily in the future when the baggage of the past keeps banging away at the trap door of our minds demanding attention." You see, how can we begin to heal, how can we begin to seek relief, if we do not first acknowledge the basis of our pain, if we do not acknowledge our guilt?

You may think that my story of guilt is just a little thing, but let me tell you it is real. We are all guilty at some time, of something. We are guilty people. We are guilty of bad thoughts, false statements, and hurtful deeds. But most of all we are guilty before a pure and holy God. We have sinned. We have fallen short of God's perfect ideal. And you know what? The Devil uses guilt against us. He accuses us. He even makes us believe his accusations. He makes us feel the pain. Sometimes that feeling of guilt you feel is justified, and sometimes it is not. But regardless, it must be dealt with. It must be cast out.

The kind of guilt I am talking about here most often has to do with what we perceive to be our part in any given tragedy; what we did or did not do. Or, more often than not it has to do with how or how we did not treat our loved one when he or she was still with us. And let me tell you, this type of thinking is foolishness! It will accomplish nothing. It is coming purely from the Devil.

Last week I told my confirmation class (I am filling in for our youth pastor that is on medical leave) that guilt will eat you up. We are studying the Apostles' Creed, and I asked them, "If guilt is so devastating, then what do you do with it?" I told them you send it to the cross. You take it to the cross. You leave it at the cross, where Christ has already dealt with it. That is what you must do with your guilt. Simply get rid of it.

Is it simple? No. It tries to hold on. It tries to cling to you. And so you need to be persistent. Send it away. Send it away over, and over, and over again, because Christ has already died for it. Christ has already defeated it at the cross.

My guilt has overwhelmed me like a burden too heavy to bear.
Psalm 38:4

We set our hearts at rest in his presence
whenever our hearts condemn us.
For God is greater than our hearts, and he knows everything.
1 John 3:20

Prayer: Deliver me from guilt.

Merciful Father, you sent your only begotten Son to die for my sins and to deliver me from all guilt and punishment. And yet I am often plagued with guilt. Forgive me.

Merciful Father, we are all guilty of sin, but Jesus has taken that sin from me. Yet the Devil accuses me, and often makes me believe his lies. He makes me feel my pain which Jesus suffered for me. Merciful Father, help me to deal with it. Help me to cast it out. Help me to get rid of it. Help me, Merciful Father, to send it to the cross where Christ has already dealt with it. Merciful Father, I pray that you set my heart at rest. In Jesus Name. Amen.

FORGIVENESS: Just as fear and worry go hand-in-hand, so does guilt and forgiveness. Guilt is pretty easy for us to understand. But it is hard to deal with. It is persistent and hard to get rid of, but we know that it must be conquered. Forgiveness on the other hand is more deceptive. Sometimes we just do not want to forgive, and sometimes we just find it hard to accept forgiveness.

Webster defines forgive as to give up claim to compensation or retaliation; to pardon. And, as I sit here and look at these words, my mind is working overtime. Jack McCullough took the precious life of my innocent little sister Maria. There is no possible compensation that could ever be offered for that horrible crime. So I guess that leaves me with retaliation or pardon. Or does it?

My mother and father struggled with this from the very beginning. They were angry, especially my mother, and she just could not let it go. I remember about twenty years ago I was leading a mid-day Bible study at our church. In the news that day there was an article about Jeffrey Dahmer and the atrocities that he had committed. The discussion turned to whether or not he could ever be forgiven. My mother said, "I could never forgive whoever killed Maria."

Later, after some years, I don't know exactly when, my father came to terms with this. When it was suggested to him that the case had been solved he said, "What difference does it make?" He had moved on. He had put his anger behind. I remember at one point he had said, "It is probably a good thing that they did not catch the guy because we would have lynched him." But thank God he had been led beyond that. Call it what you like; but he had moved on.

It was different for my mother. She needed more help. Shortly after that afternoon Bible study, I convinced her to talk with someone. Pastor Henry Dequin was very dear to us. He had helped me through some difficult times in my life, and he had also been a great encouragement to me when I finally decided to return to my studies for the ministry. My mother loved and trusted him, and agreed for counseling with her struggle with forgiveness. And here again, I thank God for using Pastor Dequin as an instrument in bringing the all-powerful healing of forgiveness to my mother.

Now, I, on the other hand, did not struggle with this. It never came into my mind. Until…Until fifty plus hears later when I was told that Jack McCullough, whom I knew as Johnny Tessier, had killed Maria. It was when a face, a person I had known, was placed on the person that kidnapped, raped, and murdered my sister that I began to struggle with forgiveness.

Sometimes I think that we as Christians get confused by that word *forgiveness*. We say, we know, that all sins, all the sins of all the people for all the time have been forgiven in Christ Jesus. But does that mean that God forgave, that he gave up claim to compensation or retaliation? Does that mean he pardoned even the smallest of sin? No. He did not. He punished sin. He placed his full wrath upon his only begotten Son Jesus as a substitute for the sinner.

Jesus said, "*If you forgive men when they sin against you, your heavenly Father will also forgive you. But if you do not forgive men their sins, your Father will not forgive your sins.*" Matthew 6:14-15. Well, just what does this mean? Jesus died for my sins once and for all. They have been forgiven in him. There was and there is nothing I could or can do to save myself from my sin, so God did it all for me. So what does this mean? Am I forgiven or not?

Jesus takes our sin upon himself as a free gift of salvation. But if you refuse to let go of it, if you refuse to let him take it, if you hold on to it, who does it belong to? Often times we are just not ready or willing to forgive. But, just like our Heavenly Father, when we forgive we are not pardoning; we are not making light of the evil act. We are not saying it is OK. But God knows how devastating un-forgiveness can be, and when we let go of it we become the recipient of God's blessing.

In August of 2008 I preached a sermon on forgiveness. In that sermon I dealt with the command given to us concerning our need to forgive those that trespass against us. I talked about how hard that often is for us to do, or perhaps, not only difficult to do, but sometimes it seems to be impossible. But, none the less, the Bible makes it clear that we must forgive. And the good news is that for those of us that at times find that so difficult to do, God also shows us why it is so important.

In the Gospel of St. Matthew (18:21) we have a brief exchange between Peter and Jesus about the extent of forgiveness. Peter says, "Lord, how often should I forgive? As many as seven times?" Here we find Peter, as we often find ourselves, looking for a way out of those commands which are so difficult for us. But Jesus' answer is straight to the point; it cannot be denied: "Not seven times, but, I tell you, seventy-seven times." Seventy-seven meaning limitless.

Well, I would like you to think about this; if forgiveness is unlimited, how can you and I ever hope to live up? We just do not have the capability do we? But forgiveness is absolute. Forgiveness must be given. And praise God that he is the one that forgives in Christ Jesus. Yes. Only God can live up to the limitless standard of forgiveness. It is God's job to forgive.

Jesus said, *"If you forgive men when they sin against you, your heavenly Father will also forgive you. But if you do not forgive men their sins, your Father will not forgive your sins."* Here again I ask, just what does this mean? Are we to understand that forgiveness is a task which we must perform in order to be forgiven? If that is true, then what about the work of Christ at the cross? It just doesn't fit does it? And, if it doesn't fit, or if it is something that we cannot understand, then we must turn to that which God has made perfectly clear to us.

Jesus took all of our sins upon himself and suffered the punishment that we deserved. It is a done deal. It is a fee gift to us to either accept or to refuse. That we know as fact. So then why the need for us to forgive others? It is because God only wants that which is good for us, and when we are unable to forgive we hold on to the baggage which comes with it. You see, in order for us to have the blessings which come with God's forgiveness we must get rid of that which blocks us from receiving them. Forgiving and forgiveness are God things, God's gifts to us, and I am thankful for that. I am thankful because it is only through forgiving and forgiveness that I am able to move on.

Do not say, "I'll pay you back for this wrong!"
Wait for the Lord, and he will deliver you.
Proverbs 20:22

Prayer: Help me understand forgiveness.

Our Father who art in heaven, forgive us our trespasses, as we forgive those who trespass against us. Father, as I pray these words, I know your will, and yet, I often struggle. Father, forgive me. Sometimes I know that it is hard for some to accept your forgiveness, and for that I pray for them. I know of my forgiveness and for that I am thankful. But sometimes I do not want to forgive others. Father, forgive me.

Father there have been times when I just could not forgive, and I needed to be led beyond. I needed to move on, and you delivered me. I needed the all-powerful healing of forgiveness, and you showed me that forgiveness only comes through Christ Jesus. You showed me that forgiveness is your work. You showed me that only you can offer complete and total forgiveness, because Jesus has satisfied your wrath. I thank you.

Father, now I pray that you enable me to not put limits on your forgiveness. I pray that you enable me to rejoice in my forgiveness, and to also rejoice in the forgiveness of others. In Jesus Name. Amen.

WHY: Why? We just need to know why. It seems to be in our nature. And when something is beyond our comprehension, when there appears to be no explanation, we just can't accept that. We want to know why. We cry out, "God, why?"

Well, you might not be ready for this, and I thought about easing into it but decided to just say it. When tragedy strikes we so often make that question of why too difficult. We know why. If it is good it comes from God. If it is bad it does not; it comes from evil.

We can just beat ourselves up with that question why even though the answer is so clear. Evil happens in an evil world. And yet, we hurt so badly and we just cannot understand why. Why my sister? Why my family? Why me? Or, how could this happen to anyone? And then eventually it comes down to the question, "Why would a loving God allow this to happen?" We are flooded with whys.

One Bible passage comes to my mind: *For my thoughts are not your thoughts, neither are your ways my ways, declares the Lord. As the heavens are higher than the earth, so are my ways higher than your ways and my thoughts than your thoughts. Isaiah 55:8-9.* This Bible message tells us that God's thinking and God's way of doing things are different than ours. But is it telling us that his thoughts and actions are beyond our understanding? No. I don't think so. This passage is giving us a glimpse of who God is, and that who he is determines how he thinks and how he acts. God is love. God is holy. God is perfect. Therefore, God is incapable of any evil. He can only do that which is good. *The fear of the Lord* (The understanding of the Lord) *is the beginning of wisdom. Psalm 111:10.*

In the Book of Job, the third chapter, Job begins by cursing the day he was born. He said, "May the day of my birth perish...May it turn to darkness...May blackness overwhelm its light." Then he goes on to ask why. Over and over he asks why. He ends that chapter by saying, "I have no peace, no quietness; I have no rest, but only turmoil."

On the anniversary of 911, that dreadful day of terror, I preached a sermon, much like I can imagine was being preached in churches throughout the country, on why do terrible things happen? A question that many asked on that horrible day, and a question that many continue to ask today. Why do terrible things happen?

Your hear it all the time, "If there really is a loving God then how could he allow so much evil to happen in this world." There has been book after book written about why bad things happen. We pray all the time to our Almighty God, and if you really believe that to be true, that he is almighty, then it only stands to reason that we would wonder why he allows so much hurt and pain to enter this world of his. And when we do we are simply saying that it is God's fault.

We all struggled with this issue. We ask, "Why did God take my son before he even had a chance to live?" We ask, "Why did God let Johnny kidnap and murder my little sister?" We ask, "Why does God let my father beat my mother?" We ask, "Doesn't God care?" We ask and we ask. We blame and we blame. And where does it get us?

When evil strikes we all want to know why? When evil strikes we all want someone to blame. Remember after 911? The flames were not yet extinguished, and the body count continued to rise, when there were those that said that we as a people of the United States were being punished by God. Many said we were being punished for the evil lives in which we had become accustomed to living. Yes. How quick we are to say that when something bad happens it is because we had it coming. Remember Job from the Bible? He was faithful to God, and when his life was turned upside down by tragedy after tragedy that is what his friends said to him. Yes, when tragedy strikes, people want to know why? They want someone to blame.

Well, as we look for answers and for someone to blame, it almost always comes down to God and who he is. And this is unfortunately true of believers and non-believers alike. And you know what? That would be just fine if when we did so we were truly looking to God and to who he is. The problem comes in when we don't. The problem comes in when we simply blame God. Yes. We blame the One who is incapable of anything which is other than good. We blame the Blameless for evil.

When bad things happen, when tragedy strikes, we do need to look at God. We need to look at who he is and what he has done. When he created us and all things, it was good, especially us, we were very good. There was nothing but good. Did you hear that? God created nothing but good.

So what happened? It was sin. God gave us the freedom of choice. He wanted us to love him as he loved us, unconditionally. Therefore, we had to be able to choose, and some of the angels along with Adam and Eve made the wrong choice. Sin entered the world, and with sin came that which is bad. With sin came murder, war, strife, famine, natural disasters, all that is bad. The perfect human race that God had created and the world in which we live was changed. And this changed world is now the reality in which we live. So, who is to blame?

Is this our eternal fate? Or can things change again? If there is indeed a loving God why doesn't he do something? What is he waiting for? Saint Peter answers that question when he said, "The Lord is not slow about his promise, but he is patient toward you, not wishing for any to perish, but for all to come to repentance." (2 Peter 3:9) Our Heavenly Father created us to be with him in everlasting bliss forever, and in Christ Jesus that will of his will be done. In fact, the victory has already been won, but the fulfillment is yet to come. You see, he wants all to be saved. He wants all to be delivered from this evil world in which we live. And when the time is right, Jesus will come again in all his glory bringing an end to this world of sin and corruption in which we live. He loves us so much that he patiently waits, even as it pains him to see us suffer now, so that we might be with him in paradise.

When tragedy strikes we need to look to God. We need to recognize who he is and what he has done. He did not bring darkness into this world of ours. We are the guilty ones. But God has even remedied that. He has taken our guilt upon himself at the cross. God is not capable of anything bad, and yet we wonder. We wonder why. We wonder how. We ask what if this and what if that. My sister Kay thought she had it all figured out. My sister Pat wants all her questions answered. My parents wanted someone to blame. I did not care about knowing everything. We are all different. But for me this is what is important. I must know God's ways and God's thoughts, for that is the beginning of understanding. Knowing God relieves me of that nagging question why? Because the outcome is far better.

Evil struck my family. An evil act from a deranged man. He kidnaped, raped, and murdered my little sister. It was an act of pure evil. But in the midst of that evil stood God, and God prevailed. Jesus, our Lord and Savior, held Maria in his arms and gently took her home to heaven. And here, in my pain, he is also. And he helps me to understand that to be with him is better by far.

> *The Lord will rescue me from every evil attack and*
> *will bring me safely to his heavenly kingdom.*
> *2 Timothy 4:18*

Prayer: Knowing God answers the question why?

Blessed Lord God, you have shown us your great love at the cross of Christ Jesus. You have also shown us the result of evil in this world. Yes. At the cross we see what kind of world we have and what kind of God. A world that chooses injustice, and a God that chooses love. And yet we continue to wonder why evil and tragedy plague us. And we continue to blame you. Forgive us. Some say all suffering and evil are paybacks from you. Some say that you do not exist. Some say that life is meaningless. Some say that you do not have the power to do anything about it. Blessed Lord God, forgive us.

Blessed Lord God, my question of why leads to no peace, no quietness, no rest; only turmoil. Evil and suffering are real. I need to know that it is OK to grieve, and it is OK to be angry. I need to realize that evil and suffering are part of the reality of the world we live in. But

I must also know that in Christ Jesus the victory has been won and that you patiently wait for us to accept that victory. I need to know that in the midst of evil, there you stand, and there you prevail. Help me, Blessed Lord God, to understand, for your ways and your thoughts are different from ours, and yet they are not beyond my understanding.

Blessed Lord God, I pray that you ever keep me mindful of who you are. I pray that I see your love in all things. I pray that my knowledge of you as revealed in Christ Jesus would relieve me of that nagging question of why? Amen.

ANGER: Earlier I said that Jesus showed us that suffering and evil are real. And he gave us permission to grieve and be angry because of them. Jesus took suffering and evil seriously and so should we. Do we have a right to be angry when evil shatters our somewhat peaceful lives? Yes we do. But in saying that I want you to know that you must be oh so very careful with that! You see anger is such a powerful emotion, and it is an emotion which can so easily backfire on us. It is contagious, and it can spread like a wildfire. You have seen it on the streets haven't you; as we see how anger turns into riots, and riots, which may have started with some righteous anger, quickly turn into the most-vile of things. And if you are anything like me, I am sure that you have seen it blacken your heart as well. That is why the Bible cautions us about our anger. The Bible says, *Refrain from anger and turn from wrath; do not fret, it leads only to evil. Psalm 37:8.* We are not to fret over our anger, which simply means that we are not to let it gnaw away at us. We are not to let it wear us down. After all, who is injured by our anger? What good does it do? Where does it lead?

We all experience anger at certain times in our lives, and even though the Bible cautions against it, anger is not forbidden. It is not in and of itself sinful. In fact it can be a healthy response to that which is bad, that evil that often attacks us. The fact is some anger is sinful, some is not.

Saint Paul writes this: *In your anger do not sin. Do not let the sun go down while you are still angry, and do not give the devil a foothold. Ephesians 4:26.* "In your anger." In other words you are going to experience anger.

That is not the problem. The problem comes when you allow your anger to take over; when it leads to sin. And let me tell you, anger can and will lead to sin if you allow it to take control. All kinds of sin. Anger becomes a problem when it separates you from that which is good. It becomes a problem when it separates or brings a barrier between you and God.

"Do not let the sun go down while you are still angry." Here we are told in such simple and practical terms to not let your anger fester. Let it alert you that something is wrong. And then move on. Just do not let it hang on! "Do not give the Devil a foothold."

In December of 2003 I had the opportunity to preach on the Devil. I told the congregation that while many today deny the reality of the devil as a personal being, the fact is he is real. He is active, and they don't call him the Deceiver for nothing, and his greatest deception is to have you believe he is not real. You see, once he has you believing he is not real he has you approaching his lure. He will use whatever means available to snare you, and usually we provide the means.

Well, there can be no doubt that one of those means is anger, and anger can give Satan a foothold in us. Anger can give Satan a starting place to not simply frustrate us, but to use that frustration to take us down a dangerous path. I hope that you firmly believe in the Devil. I hope that you know that the Devil will use whatever means available to separate you from the love of God. And you must be careful because the Devil will take that anger of yours and he will use it against you. He will use it to isolate you from the healing that you so desperately need. Think about it. Listen to the warning. Jesus said, "How foolish you are." And Jesus has shown us how crafty Satan, the Deceiver, can be. We simply must put our frustrations, our foolishness, and most of all our anger aside. Yes. We must listen to the warning.

A fool gives full vent to his anger.
Proverbs 29:11

Prayer: Do not let my anger fester.

Almighty God, Author of life and health, you want only that which is good for me, and I know that you will deliver me from evil. I trust in your life giving power and your healing strength. Almighty God, I praise you.

But suffering and evil are real. I often struggle with anger, and sometimes my anger backfires on me. My anger often gnaws away at me. My anger often wears me down. My anger often takes over. My anger often blinds me, and the Devil often uses it against me. Almighty God, Author of life and health, give me strength; relieve me of my foolishness.

Almighty God, I ask for your forgiveness when I succumb to my anger. Almighty God, I ask for strength and deliverance from the Evil One. I pray that you not let my anger blacken my heart. I pray that you not let my anger separate me from that which is good. Almighty God, Author of life and health, I pray that you not let the Devil get a foothold in me. I pray that you not let my anger hang on. I pray that you enable me to put my anger aside. Amen.

ANXIETY/DEPRESSION: My mother lost her mother when she was a young girl of seventeen. A few years later, as a young bride, she lost her first husband after one year of marriage. And then she loses her youngest child in such a horrible way, kidnaped and murdered. My mother struggled with anxiety and depression for many years. In fact, on that first Christmas Eve, just three weeks after Maria was taken, my mother, in a fit of hysteria, threatened to take all of her pills and kill herself. On a night in which Christians everywhere were celebrating, our household was filled with the shadow of gloom and depression. Depression was something that my mother struggled with for most of her life.

We went through the motions of that first Christmas without Maria.
Chuck is holding the pogo-stick Maria had asked Santa to bring.

I, on the other hand, was not overwhelmed with anxiety or depression. I have certainly had some low spots in my life, many or even most of which I have brought upon myself, but I am thankful that God has always lifted me up above them. I think that depression can set in when your mind is filled with thoughts that are depressing. Why do we do that? Why do we let the gloom take over? Maybe it is because some of us just like being depressed. As outrageous as that sounds, I believe it is true. Some of us just like being depressed. Even those that are sick of always being plagued with depression, those that desperately want to be lifted out of that pit, many just cannot help themselves. Many just cannot get out of bed. Some know what they must or should do. Some know of the help that is available to them. But they just cannot take that first step to recovery.

I can remember back in the eighties when I owned this bar, Beak's Place in Virgil. The guys, or sometimes even the gals, when they were a little down they would come in and drink and play what they would call *sad songs.* Perhaps when they had broken-up with a girl-friend or boy-friend they would play the saddest country & western songs they could find on the juke box. The more they drank, and the more sad songs they played, the better, or the sadder, I am not sure which, they felt. It almost seemed like the sadder they were, and the sadder they helped others to feel, the better it was. And this is how we can be as well when dealing with anxiety or depression. But I have to ask, why in the world would we do this?

Well, I think it is important, very important, sometimes even life and death important, for us to realize that there are times when we just cannot help ourselves! And this may be true of all of these emotions and feelings that we will go through, but it is especially important for anxiety and depression.

I am so thankful that when I was, and often still am, troubled with any of these powerful feelings, that I know enough to seek help. And it is all important for you to know that help is at hand. For me help came from many different fronts; yes different fronts, but all of which I know were sent by God.

In my journal on September 14, 2012, I wrote: "Pat and I had great support throughout...Bill & Diane, cousins Betty Jo & Bonnie, Maria, Nani, Ken, Bill, Rod, Aggie, James, Karen & Nancy, along with the Hickey boys and many others!" Yes, God brought our loved ones front and center to do what they do best; to love us.

God put Pastor Koester, Father Paul, Pastor Weinhold, and Pastor Dequin into my life to council and to comfort. God put Peter Henderson, Emily Wichick, and Charles Lachman, caring strangers in our lives, to walk beside us. And most of all, at least for me, God reminded me of his great love over and over as the Holy Spirit kept me in faith. The Holy Spirit overcame with his promptings and reminders of all the promises which are ours in Christ Jesus. And for those of us that need something more tangible, something medical, God provides professional psychologists and psychiatrists to help us and guide us through. The important thing is to not reject the help which is available to us.

I was at an AA gathering several years ago and there was this speaker from New York City that was talking about accepting help. You see, in AA just as anywhere else, so many reject help from some sources for a variety of reasons. He said, "Why in the world would you reject anything that might help you?" And that question holds true for us all. "Why in the world would you reject anything that might help you?"

> Then they cried to the Lord in their trouble, and
> he saved them from their deep distress.
> He brought them out of darkness and the deepest
> gloom and broke away their chains.
> Psalm 107:13-14

Prayer: Lead me out of depression.

O Father of mercies and God of all comfort, you said, "Let there be light." And there was light. Father, you did not create me to live in darkness and gloom, and yet, that is where I often find myself. God of all comfort, our house was filled with the shadow of gloom and depression. This was not your will for me, and you delivered me. I thank you. O Father of mercies, you have always lifted me up, and I thank you. But still I often fill my mind with depressing thoughts; still I often let gloom take over. Forgive me. It seems that there are times when I just cannot help myself.

But, Father of mercies and God of all comfort, I have seen, I have experienced your helping hand. I know that you provide all the help which I need, and I praise you. I pray now that you enable me to recognize the help that you send. I pray that you enable me to seek help when it is needed. I pray that you do not allow me to reject help as it is offered. I pray that you take me by my hand and lead me out of the darkness and the gloom. In Jesus Name, and by the power of the Holy Spirit. Amen.

REVENGE: I don't know about you, but I just hate that word *revenge*. It makes me think that such a word has no place in our vocabulary. But here it is, and for something that should not exist it certainly is active in our world today, and perhaps even in our own lives.

Webster's Dictionary defines revenge as to inflict harm or injury in return; to exact satisfaction. I have to wonder, and I hope you do as well, if any satisfaction is achieved by revenge? And I also hope that you agree with me that to injure or to harm someone else would simply cause me nothing but pain. And yet, we as a people often relish revenge. Revenge can affect us all in one way or another, and it does not have to be as severe as wanting, even praying for our offender to be executed for his or her offense. It could be something less radical, perhaps something like no longer talking to a family member because of something they have done. Both of which can be harmful, to ourselves and to those around us.

I thank God that for me revenge has not been a major issue, and heaven knows I did not need some other major emotion playing havoc with my mind. Yes. I wanted Jack McCullough tried and convicted for what he had done to my sister Maria, but my thoughts were never driven by the need for his punishment. Before the sentencing, in my impact statement to the judge, I asked that the verdict make a bold statement to all that we as a society will not tolerate such evil crimes against our children. I went on to say, "I ask that you pronounce the maximum sentence allowed under the law; not out of revenge, but for justice, justice for Maria, and justice for our community. The maximum punishment says that we will protect our children, and we will punish those who bring them harm. I ask that the sentence which you pronounce shouts out with a clear voice that those who abuse and murder our children will be punished to the full extent of the law". I am thankful that what happened to Jack McCullough for the evil act that he committed did not really matter. What mattered to me most was the message that we as a community were putting out to a world which seems to be so calloused against evil.

Jack McCullough was given the maximum sentence available under the law, but for me there was no reason to celebrate. Was I happy with the judge's decision? Yes. But it brought no comfort, no satisfaction. And now, four years later, after he has been released because of some perceived flaw in the trial, does it matter? Yes. But not because of the fact that my revenge has not been satisfied, but because of the message which needed to be sent has been compromised.

When someone has wronged you so deeply that your whole life has been changed and simply appears to have gotten away with it, it is like you have been hurt all over again. It is simply our human nature to want them to pay for what they have done. But let me ask you, who does it hurt when you seek revenge? Revenge is simply a place where you do not want to go. Revenge is simply a word which does not belong in our vocabulary. When tragedy strikes it brings with it great pain, but revenge will bring with it only more darkness, a darkness which can and should be avoided.

Do not seek revenge or bear a grudge.
Leviticus 19:18

Do not seek revenge.

Most Righteous and Ever-Living God, you are the Judge over all things and in all places. And yet I often try to take your place. Forgive me. You have shown me your great mercy and I thank you. I have often offended you, and I often harmed those around me, and yet you graciously forgive me for Christ sake. I praise you.

Most Righteous and Ever-Living God, when I am wronged, I often seek revenge. I often cry out for punishment. Help me, Most Righteous God, to not go there. Help me to stay away from the attitude of revenge which only leads me into dark places. I pray for strength so that I do not seek revenge or bear a grudge. Amen.

HOPE: On Friday, December 6, 1957, three days after my sister Maria was kidnaped, my sisters Pat, Kay, and I went back to school. My sister Kay wrote in her diary: "I felt like Exhibit A all day. One of my teachers stopped me in the hall and asked if there was anything new in the case. Then she had the nerve to say 'You've lost all hope, haven't you?'"

When my father returned to work a few days after Maria was taken he responded to his co-workers greetings by saying, "I'm almost positive Maria will be found dead. The only thing you can do is to teach your kids to be more careful." And for me, upon returning to school, I just did not know what to say. Well, this is what I have to say about it now. We all, the entire town feared the worst. But fearing the worst and giving up hope are entirely two different things!

Webster defines hope as desire with expectation of obtaining what is desired or belief that it is obtainable; trust; reliance. I am just sitting here and trying to figure out how to describe how our Christian hope fits in with this secular definition. I tell people all the time that for us as Christians our hope is more than a "pie-in-the-sky" kind of hope. Our hope is a certainty. And yet, even though we did not expect Maria to be found alive, we were not without hope. How can that be?

During those first days that Maria was missing, we certainly had real hope that she would be returned to us unharmed. But as days, and weeks, and months went by, that changed. The reality of the fact that it was unlikely that she would be found alive had set in. We were even faced with the possibility that she might not ever be found. But were we left hopeless? Never!

For us as Christians hope is a certainty! We may not know how any given situation is going to play out, but whatever it is; whatever the outcome, we are not left hopeless. I continue to look at that definition from Webster and it just does not give me the answer I am looking for. I want to share with you what I know for certain, but just cannot find the words. And so, as I always do, or at least as I always should do, I am going to turn to the Lord and what he tells us about this certainty of hope. *We have this hope as an anchor for the soul, firm and secure. Hebrews 6:19.*

I often talk about our hope as a Christian, and I have often preached on it. In July of 2014 I quoted the above Bible passage saying that since we have a living hope in Jesus Christ, our souls are anchored, moored, and fastened to him in heaven. Yes, we have an anchor for our soul, like an anchor holding a ship safely in its place. And that anchor reaches up into heaven. Our hope is in Christ who is seated at the right hand of God the Father himself. Though all the tragedies and the evil of this world rage against us, though we may be led along many a dark path, though we may be confronted with fear and doubt, we have Christ as the anchor for our souls. And nothing, absolutely nothing, can snatch us out of his hand. In this is the certainty of our hope.

Without hope we have nothing. What is there to life without hope? Is this all there is; this life filled with tragedy and pain? Is our only hope death and then the end? What kind of hope is that? Well, for you and for me we do have hope. We have been to the empty tomb and have seen the victory in Christ Jesus. Yes, you and I can lift up our eyes and see the glory of God. We can lift up our eyes and see beyond this sinful world of pain. All is not lost. The best is yet to come.

You see, we feared that Maria's life here on earth had been taken from us, but we were not deprived of our hope. All was not lost. No one could take her out of the loving arms of Jesus. You see, for me my hope is bigger and broader than for those without faith. For me my hope begins at the top. I see the overall picture. I know that I cannot lose, because the greatest gift, the greatest hope has already been fulfilled.

Job, a person of great faith, lost what the world would consider everything. He lost his family, his possessions, and his health, and yet he had this to say about God: *Though he slay me, yet will I hope in him. Job 13:15.* You see, no matter what plagues us in this life, we have so much more to look forward to in the life to come. And that does not always mean that we must wait for this life to end before our hopes are fulfilled. Job was again richly blessed in this life. But whatever may come, this we know, the victory has been won. The victory is ours in Christ Jesus.

Listen to this: *I remember my affliction and my wandering, the bitterness and the gall. I well remember them, and my soul is downcast within me. Yet this I call to mind and therefore I have hope: Because of the Lord's great love we are not consumed, for his compassions never fail. They are new every morning... I will wait for him. The Lord is good to those whose hope is in him, to the one who seeks him.* Lamentations 3:19-25.

I remember the pain; the sense of loss. I remember the realization that Maria was gone. But I was never hopeless. I was not consumed. If it were not for hope our hearts would break beyond repair. Yes, as bad as things are we are not consumed because of God's grace.

In my journal under the theme of *God is here. I have joyously discovered that he is always up to something' in my life, and I am learning to quit second-guessing him and simply trust the process.* There I wrote: "March 24, 2013. Preached at Hampshire this morning. Yesterday Maria invited us to come up for Chase's birthday & so we drove up after church. Yes, God is always up to something in my life." "March 28, 2013. Had lunch with Sycamore Police Chief Don Thomas today. He has been so supportive throughout everything surrounding Maria's case." "March 30, 2013. Went to Dixon Prison today and as usual it was uplifting to be with men sharing our faith in those circumstances." "March 31, 2013. It is Easter and Maria came down to join us all for dinner. Yes. God is always up to something in my life! And I give him thanks."

The next theme in my journal was from Jeremiah 29:11. *For I know the plans I have for you, declares the Lord, plans to prosper you and not to harm you, plans to give you hope and a future."* There I wrote: "April 6, 2013. Maria called. They were in St. Charles for the flea market and wanted to meet us for a late lunch. How Great!" "April 12, 2013. Had breakfast with a friend from AA. I think I was able to help him. I know he helped me." Yes. "Plans to give you hope and a future."

May the God of hope fill you with all joy and peace as you trust in him.
Romans 15:13

Prayer: May the Holy Spirit fill me with hope.

O God of love and grace, you give me all things including the certainty of hope, and I praise you. You have given me the gift of knowing that my hope is firm and secure, and I thank you. Yes, whatever the outcome I am not left hopeless. Yes, my hope is bigger and broader because it is anchored in Christ; it begins at the top, and I know that I cannot lose because the greatest hope has already been fulfilled. I thank you, and I praise you, O God of love and grace.

O Lord, I pray that you continue to show me your love and your grace so that I know that no matter what plagues me in this life, I have so much more to look forward to in the life to come. O God of love and grace, I know that without hope my life would be miserable, aimless, and without meaning. I know that without hope my heart would break beyond repair. Therefore I pray for hope. I pray that you enable me to see that you have something in store for me. I pray that you enable me to envision my future filled with your love and your grace. Yes, I pray that the Holy Spirit fill me with hope. Amen.

Two days ago, Sunday, April 17, 2016, two days after a judge set aside the conviction of Jack McCullough for the murder of my sister Maria, I preached at the Trinity Lutheran Church in Hampshire, Illinois. As I welcomed the congregation I said, "Jesus is alive and present among us." I said, "How important that fact is to each one of us. Jesus is alive and present, right now and always, and will guide us to streams of living water and wipe away every tear from our eyes." We then went on to sing over and over, "On Christ, the solid rock, I stand; all other ground is sinking sand." We prayed, "Lord, our Good Shepherd, enemies confront us daily, enemies of the cross, emissaries of Satan, who would work to hinder any good work, who would weaken our spirits, who would seek to increase our despair, enemies who would attack our health, our families, our values, and our faith, and yet in the very presence of these real enemies, you are there. You prepare a table before us. You anoint our heads with oil. Our cup overflows." And then we sang, "Lord, take my hand and lead me upon life's way; direct, protect, and feed me from day to day. Without your grace and favor I go astray; so take my hand, O Savior, and lead the way."

Then, as I began to preach, I told the congregation that I had gotten up early, as was my custom when I would be leading worship, so that I would have ample time to ponder and meditate upon the message I was about to be delivering. I said that this morning was different. I found it hard to focus. My thoughts kept drifting away from the hope that I was about to proclaim to the darkness which wanted to engulf me. I told the congregation I was struggling with the Devil as he tried to interfere with Jesus' message of hope.

I then brought us all, myself included, into the present as I said how I liked the season of Spring; new life, new hopes, and new dreams. I talked about the certainty of the hope which is ours in Christ Jesus. I spoke of how the Devil is constantly plotting to rob us of our faith. I said, "All around us is a world full of attractions and distractions which tend to draw us away from the Savior and to make us forget those things which are most important. Add to this our own weakness as we face each and every day, and we must realize that left to our own devices there would be little hope. In fact, there would be no hope at all. Don't you see, this world of ours is the Devil's play-ground. Even God's good gifts he uses against us to draw us away from our Lord rather than praising him for all that he gives us. Yes, the temptations of the Devil are very appealing, and the allurements, and the distractions of the world very powerful. And by our own strength we could never hold out against them."

Then I said, "But the truth is it is just this knowledge of our weakness that points us to the Lord. Yes. We are weak, but he is strong. Though this life may seem unbearable, we have hope in the strength of the Lord. No matter how bad it may seem, no one, absolutely nothing, can overcome the victory which has already been won in Christ Jesus our Lord." Now that is a certain hope! A hope which is ours in Christ Jesus.

Find rest, O my soul, in God alone; my hope comes from him.
Psalm 62:5

Prayer: May I find hope in my weakness.

Eternal and Everlasting Father, I thank you for revealing your presence, right here and right now, in Christ Jesus, my Lord, and my God. I thank you for the promise that you will lead me to streams of living water; that you will wipe away the tears from my eyes. But Satan attacks me. Satan entices me. Satan often steals my rest.

I pray, Eternal and Everlasting Father, for you to take my hand. Lead me. Direct me. Protect me. Satan tries to deceive me. He would have me believe there is not hope. I pray for you to bring me into the present, into the season of new life, new hopes, and new dreams. I pray, let my hope be in your strength. Amen.

PEACE: Is it a surprise to anyone that we live in a world of sin, a world that appears to be in complete turmoil? Murder, war, strife, everywhere. People, even parents and children killing each other. Wars are being fought all over the world, and even in our own country, we've adopted a terror alert system. A system that while unheard of a few years ago, is now part of our national vocabulary. Well, in light of all this how do we find real peace?

Jesus said, "In this world you will have trouble. But take heart! I have overcome the world." (John 16:33) These words of Jesus in the Gospel of St. John came just hours before He would be crucified, and the lives of the disciples would be rocked to their very foundations. You see, soon the Messiah they had hoped for and believed in would die a horrible death, and they would live in fear for their own lives. Jesus, anticipating this, and also the persecution to come after His resurrection, looks to put their minds at ease with these words: "I have told you these things, so that in me you may have peace. In this world you will have trouble. But take heart! I have overcome the world."

You listen to the news and you read the newspapers and what do you see? And then you hear of how this political leader is going to do this, and how that leader is going to do that to change things. Does it get better? My wife Diane says it will never get better. And you know what? She is right. Just as Jesus said, "In this world you will have trouble." But he didn't leave it there did he? No. He said, "In me you may have peace." He said, "Take heart! I have overcome the world."

The turmoil of this world is all around us. Does time eliminate the turmoil? No. Time may change it, but for me it has just kept coming, only in different forms. Yes. The turmoil changes, but thanks be to God that so do we. We change, and the way in which we face the turmoil can change as well. How do we change? For the better? Or, for the worse? Will the turmoil prevail, or will you find peace?

Jesus said, "In me you may have peace."

It has been said that the average person has more than two hundred negative thoughts a day; worries, jealousies, insecurities, cravings for forbidden things, and the list goes on and on. It has also been said that depressed people have as many as six hundred. You can't eliminate all the troublesome things that go through your mind, but you can certainly reduce the number of negative thoughts.

Next week, March 29, 2016, two days after the victory celebration of Easter, my sister Pat and I go once again into the courtroom hoping for a clear decision on Jack McCullough's latest petition. We are hoping for some finality. But we have many concerns. We lack confidence in the state's attorney's motives and his abilities. We feel victimized once again. But this is what I am doing about it: As I am bombarded with all those negative thoughts, with all that "what if" kind of thinking, I am immediately putting those thoughts out of my mind. I am trusting in Jesus words, "In me you may have peace." I know those words to be true because I have found that peace so many times before.

In the Old Testament of the Bible we are told of Gideon, a man who lived in troubled times to whom an angel of the Lord appeared. The angel said, "The Lord is with you, mighty warrior." Gideon replied, "If the Lord is with us, why has all this happened to us? Where are all his wonders? The Lord has abandoned us." The Lord turned to him and said, "Go in the strength you have and save Israel." Gideon then asked, "How can I save Israel? My clan is the weakest in Manasseh, and I am the least in my family." God gave Gideon a sign, and the Lord said to him, "Peace! Do not be afraid." So Gideon built an altar to the Lord there and called it *The Lord is Peace.* Judges 6:12-24.

"The Lord is Peace!" Gideon came face to face with the Lord, and found Peace. In the midst of great turmoil, Gideon found Peace, and so can you. Yes.   The Lord told Gideon to go in the strength he had. The strength he had, and the strength we have as well. "Peace! Do not be afraid." That is what the Lord says. Yes. The Lord is Peace.

The dictionary defines peace as a state of tranquility or quiet; freedom from fears or agitating passions; a pact or an agreement to end hostilities. The Bible's definition is more direct. The Lord is Peace.

Jesus said, "In me you may have peace." In Philippians 4:7 St. Paul writes: "And the peace of God, which transcends all understanding, will guard your hearts and your minds in Christ Jesus." This peace of God is not merely a psychological state of mind, but an inner tranquility based on peace with God. Yes, in order to find the peace of God in the midst of all the turmoil of this world, you need to put first things first. Yes, first gain peace with God, for you can't have the peace of God until you have peace with God, the peaceful state of sins forgiven.

The peace of God, being the opposite of anxiety, it is the tranquility that comes when a believer commits all his cares to God in prayer and then worries about them no more. And for me, that has been the key; to worry about them no more. And this is something that I really need to focus on. I need to give my worries to God in prayer and then trust that he will deal with them. I must come to God face to face, and like Gideon say, "Lord, you are Peace!"

"The Lord is Peace." And, you know what? The more you know the Lord the more peace you have. Several years ago my home church, St. John Lutheran in Sycamore, Illinois, burned down. It was a sad day for all of Sycamore, a church burning to the ground, but it was especially sad for those of us that had been baptized there, married there, and had seen our children baptized and married there. During that time in which my church did not have a regular place of worship we were worshiping in a school gymnasium. On Good Friday my family and I decided to visit a small church in Dixon, Illinois. The sermon was different. In fact it was not a sermon at all as we would understand sermons. The sanctuary was darkened. One word was boldly shown upon a screen: SINNER. Then a pause of several minutes for individual reflection or meditation. Then another word: FORGIVENESS. And, another pause. This process was repeated over again and again throughout the sermon time ending in prayer.

"The Lord is Peace." Are you familiar with meditation, or reflecting upon God and his great mercy? I have come to see the importance and the benefits of this practice in my life, especially when it comes to receiving, and to knowing peace. And I have found that it does not need to be complicated. Like so many gifts that the Lord gives us we have a tendency to complicate things, and often in the process we then lose out on the gift.

In that old church of mine, the one that burned down, as you entered the inner door, chiseled in the stone arch were these words: *Be still, and know that I am God.* I walked under that archway for many years, probably thousands of times, and never knew those words were there. How fitting that those words from Psalm 46:10 should be there, and also how typical it was that I had not seen them. But now those words are ever before me. *Be still, and know that I am God.*

Several years ago I came across this sermon, I don't know where it came from or who wrote it, but it moved me. It read like this:

A member of a certain church, who previously had been attending services regularly, stopped going. After a few weeks, the preacher decided to visit him. It was a chilly evening. The pastor found the man at home alone, sitting before a blazing fire. Guessing the reason for his preacher's visit, the man welcomed him, led him to a comfortable chair near the fireplace, and waited. The preacher made himself at home but said nothing. In the grave silence, he contemplated the dance of the flames around the burning logs. After some minutes, the preacher took the fire tongs, carefully picked up a brightly burning ember and placed it to one side of the hearth all alone, then he sat back in his chair, still silent. The host watched all this in quiet contemplation. As the lone ember's flame flickered and diminished, there was a momentary glow and then its fire was no more. Soon it was cold and dead. Not a word had been spoken since the initial greeting. The preacher glanced at his watch and realized it was time to leave. He slowly stood up, picked up the cold, dead ember and placed it back in the middle of the fire. Immediately it began to glow, once more with the light and warmth of the burning coals around it. As the preacher reached the door to leave, his host said with a tear running down his cheek, "Thank you so much for your visit and especially for the fiery sermon. I will be back in church next Sunday."

We live in a world today, which tries to say too much with too little. Sometimes the best sermons are the ones left unspoken.

*The Lord is my shepherd…*That is a relationship. *I shall not want…* That is supply. *He maketh me to lie down in green pastures…*That is rest. *He leadeth me beside the still waters…*That is refreshment. *He restoreth my soul…*That is healing. *He leadeth me in the paths of righteousness…* That is guidance. *For his name's sake…*That is purpose. *Yea, though I walk through the valley of the shadow of death…*That is testing. *I will fear no evil…*That is protection. *For thou art with me…*That is faithfulness. *Thy rod and thy staff comfort me…*That is discipline. *Thou prepares a table before me in the presence of mine enemies…*That is hope. *Thou annointest my head with oil…*That is consecration. *My cup runneth over…*That is abundance. *Surely goodness and mercy shall follow me all the days of my life…*That is blessing. *And I will dwell in the house of the Lord…*That is security. *Forever…*That is eternity.

What is most valuable is not what we have in our lives, but who we have in our lives. "The Lord is Peace." "Be still, and know that I am God."

Several years after that Good Friday service in Dixon, I was worshiping at the new St. John Church, and during the service we were asked to spend some time in silent reflection and meditation before confession and absolution. I closed my eyes and said, "Be still, and know that I am God." And as I said those words over and over quietly to myself my mind was filled with images of who God is and what he has done for me. My mind was filled with peace.

Today I practice this often. Sometimes I meditate upon these words in solitude, and that is a real blessing. But the beauty of these words is that I can focus on them in the midst of the greatest commotion or turmoil and instantly be reminded of who God is and what he has and will continue to do. When I stop and say, "Be still, and know that I am God" all that I know about my Lord comes rushing in. And it only stands to reason that the more we know about God; the more we search the Scriptures, his living Word, the more the Holy Spirit will reveal to us. Yes, Gideon built an altar to the Lord and called it *The Lord is Peace*. Yes, the Lord is Peace.

The Lord bless you and keep you;
The Lord make his face shine upon you and be gracious to you;
The Lord turn his face toward you and give you peace.
Numbers 6:24-26

Prayer: My Lord is peace.

O God of Peace, although we live in a sinful world so full of turmoil, yet you give me peace, for you yourself are peace. Jesus said, "You will have trouble, but in me you will have peace." And I know, I have seen that to be true. And I praise you.

O God of Peace, I can't eliminate all the troublesome things that go through my mind, but you can help me to reduce the number of my negative thoughts. And I pray for that help. Heavenly Father, God of Peace, I pray that you enable me to commit all my cares to you, and then to worry about them no more. I pray that you enable me to meditate upon you and your great mercy. I pray that you enable me to hold onto the peace which you give me. In Jesus Name. Amen.

You know, peace in this life, in this trouble world of ours is often fleeting. It often seems to come and go. But I thank God that I have learned how to have more peace than turmoil. I thank God that he has shown me where I can turn to find that peace which he gives me.

Today is Thursday, April 28, 2016, and yesterday in the paper there was an article which almost praised our state's attorney for the diligent work he had done to secure the release from prison the person convicted of killing my little sister Maria. I was irate. I wanted to lash out. I was thoroughly upset. I believed that this state's attorney had so clearly presented false assumption after false assumption which were not being challenged, and therefore were being perceived as true. I was frustrated because I had been advised by my lawyer not to speak out because that may have an adverse effect upon the testimony I was going to be required to make in court. I was asking that this state's attorney be replaced by a special prosecutor. My peace was being threatened to say the least.

But, oh how God works! Guess what the sermon topic is that I am working on for Sunday morning. The words of Jesus as he said, "I have told you these things so that in me you may have peace." WOW! You see, God's Word is filled with promises that you and I can turn to help us get through life and through the grind of day-to-day living. This message of peace given to us by Jesus is the message which I need to hear for myself today. And, therefore, it is a message that I will have no difficulty relaying to my congregation tomorrow, and sharing with you right now. You see, this message of peace is very dear to me, as it should be, and it has been a recurring theme throughout my life. Yes. All of our lives, yours and mine included are filled with uncertainty, pain, and turmoil. And for me and my family, this message of peace is something that we have prayed for. This message of peace is something that all of us hope for.

Remember as a child, how when it would thunder and lightning during the night and you would look for a place to hide? Remember how you would cover your head with the blankets looking for a place of safety? Well, that is kind of like how it is for us as we seek some sort of peace in this world filled with turmoil. And, sad to say, so many of us, perhaps all of us, look in all the wrong places. Yes. We look and we search for that quiet place of peace where nothing can disturb us. We look for some relief from the fears and the evil that surrounds us. We look for some assurance. We look for some hope. We look for some joy. We want peace. We search for it, and we pray for it, but it so often alludes us. Why we wonder? Jesus said he would give us peace, so, where is it?

Well, maybe you and I sometimes overlook the very basic. This peace which Jesus talks about, this peace which the angels announced on that first Christmas Eve was peace between God and men. You see, that is where all the evil began in the first place; when Adam and Eve sinned again God creating that barrier, causing a separation, turning peace into turmoil. So where do we find that peace that we are looking for? We need to return to God.

In Hebrew, the word peace, Shalom, is much more than the absence of things that disturb us. Peace is rather linked to the concept of wholeness, of being "at one" with God and with our neighbors, and ourselves. It is a matter of not only having an absence of war, but of having the causes of war eliminated. It is not only an absence of pain and distress, but of having the disease that causes the pain and distress cured. That is what Jesus was about when he walked among us, and what he continues to be about even today. Yes, Jesus said, "My peace I leave with you, my peace I give to you. I do not give to you as the world gives.

Do not let your hearts be troubled, and do not let them be afraid. Take heart! I have overcome the world."

I am a witness. I have seen him. I have experienced his peace. This morning my sister Pat called to see how I was holding up. I told her yesterday I was filled with anger. I was filled with frustration. I was not in a good place. Then I said, "Today I am fine. I am working on my sermon for Sunday, and Jesus has given me his promised peace."

Will I again struggle with this often fleeting peace? Yes. I am sure that I will. We face struggles all the time. The world is in turmoil all around us. But know this: The peace which Jesus promises is a peace that lasts, a peace that triumphs, a peace that heals, and that is something that the world cannot give us. It can only come to us from God.

I have told you these things, so that in me you may have peace."
John 16:33

Prayer: Jesus give me peace.

Lord God, Father, Son, and Holy Spirit, I so often get lost within myself. I so often get lost in the turmoil and seemingly injustices of this world, and I look for assurance. I look for hope. I look for joy. I look for a place where nothing can disturb me. I look for the quieting of my heart. But, Lord God, I must confess that I often do not simply turn to you. Forgive me.

Lord God, the Devil often uses those things which I cannot control to frustrate and anger me. I often want to lash out. And then, Lord God, there you are, and you quiet me. I thank you.

Lord God, Father, Son, and Holy Spirit, I now pray for that peace which is mine; that peace that lasts, that peace that triumphs, that peace which heals, and that peace which no one, not even the Devil, can take from me. Amen.

Jesus stepped into the storm of my life and said, "In me you may have peace." John 16:33. In the Psalms I am told, "I will be glad and rejoice in your love, for you saw my affliction and knew the anguish of my soul." Psalm 31:7. And Jesus said, "My joy may be in you…and your joy may be complete." John 15:11. This is how my emotions do not get the best of me. In his great love, my Lord gives me peace so that my joy may be complete.

Chapter Eight

The Results

This morning, Sunday, April 10, 2016, I was off, I was not assisting with worship, and I was not preaching at Trinity Luthcran in Hampshire, so my wife Diane and I went to St. John in Sycamore for worship. To our surprise Pastor Balgeman was the guest minister. Pastor Don Balgeman is very dear to me. He served as counselor of our circuit of Lutheran Church Missouri Synod congregations at a critical time in the beginning of my ministry. He was a major influence in the beginning of Christian Senior Ministries which I started. This was a ministry to senior residences and nursing homes in our area. He also assigned me as a lay-minister deacon to serve as an interim pastor at Trinity Lutheran in Hampshire, Illinois. That was in July of 2004, and I continue to serve that congregation today.

The past several days had been very difficult. On Good Friday morning I was informed that the state's attorney had joined forces with the defense attorneys for Jack McCullough in an all-out effort to have his conviction of the murder of my sister overturned. And the coming week was going to be equally as bad or even worse. So I was glad to see Pastor Balgeman. I came to worship expecting to be lifted up, and regardless of who was there to lead me in worship, I would have been. But just as always, God gave me more than I even expected. Yes. I was glad to see Pastor Balgeman.

Pastor Balgeman's sermon was based on Acts 9:1-22, the story of Saul the persecutor of Jesus, who became Paul, the apostle of Jesus. This is a powerful message of how people can and do change. He began by saying that just as dramatically as Saul was changed, so are we changed. Our first and foremost inclination as people is to think only evil thoughts. Many like to say that there is good in everyone. But the truth is nothing good lives within me. Now, with that being so, then why do we not succumb to that evil? Why? When I was confronted by the evil associated with the kidnapping, rape, and murder of my little sister, why did I not succumb?

Jesus. Jesus stepped in, and just like with Saul, everything changed. Yes. When Jesus enters a person's life things change. Yes. With God's intervention things change. And things changed dramatically for me when I was guided by the light of Christ rather than the darkness of the evil which surrounded me. Saul was breathing out threatenings and slaughter (KJ Version of the Bible). It came from within; he was breathing out. Yet his threatenings were changed to prayer.

I too pray. I like Saul have been changed through all that this tragedy has brought upon me. I have continued to change. I have continued to grow, to be strengthened, from the beginning right down to this very moment. You see, the evil, the Devil, comes in darkness, while Christ comes in light, for he is himself the light of the world. The Lord spoke to Saul; to him alone, and things changed. He was changed. And this same Jesus came to me, and I too was brought out of darkness into his marvelous light. Yes, this is the result. I have been brought out of the darkness into the marvelous light.

You are my lamp, O Lord; the Lord turns my darkness into light.
2 Samuel 22:29

Prayer: What a dramatic change.

Lord God, Who gives all things, I thank and praise you. As I make my way through this life, I am faced with difficult days, including today. But, Lord God, today I expect to be lifted up, and I am. Lord God, giver of all things, you always give me more good than I ever expect, and I thank and praise you for that. Jesus steps in and everything changes. Yes, with your intervention, things change.

Lord God, today I pray not only in thanksgiving for what you have done, but also for your continued intervention. I pray that as darkness continues to threaten me, that you enable me to see Jesus as he steps in. I pray that you enable me to walk in his light, and to grasp his gift of change and deliverance. Amen.

This morning I woke up early with this thought in my mind: My daughter Maria was a great inspiration to me. I just could not get that thought out of my mind, and I wanted to tell her so. I wanted to tell her she was an inspiration to me even though I knew she would not have the slightest idea of what I was talking about. You see, I had been a coward all those years of separation from her. I had never thought about that before, but I was a coward. I was afraid to deal with the pain. I hid from facing it at all cost. I was a coward. And then, after forty years, here stands this little girl, now an adult, stepping forward, displaying great courage, and saying, "I am Maria". And while I am lying in bed thinking about this, I realize that this was the moment that God had brought about to inspire me to step forward as well. This was the beginning of my great leap in faith and in trust of God.

My daughter Maria stepped into the unknown with courage. Who knows what she had been told about me, if anything. Who knows what she was thinking. But there she was. And it was this action of hers that gave me the courage to do what God now allowed me to see needed to be done. It is this one brave act which has led me to grow in faith and trust to the extent that I know God will give to me that which is good according to his gracious will.

This inspiration goes beyond my relationship with my daughter. It extends into all the problems and hurdles that I would choose to hide from each and every day. It extends to the court hearing in which I must appear in two days. I am to speak in defense of the conviction of Jack McCullough for the murder of my sister Maria, an unknown of which I am fearful, but which I can also step into with courage. Yes, this is the result of being delivered by God through all the past hurts and trials that once plagued me in the past. My daughter Maria stepped forward, and now, thank God, and with his help, so can I.

> *When they saw the courage of Peter and John...*
> *They were astonished and they took note that*
> *these men had been with Jesus.*
> *Acts 4:13*

Prayer on courage.

O Father of all, in your might, in your wisdom, and in your mercy you give all. I thank you for who you are, what you have done, and what you continue to do. Father, I was and I am often a coward. I thank you for placing in my life examples of courage, especially my daughter Maria. I thank you, Father, that you have shown me that I too can step forward in faith and in trust of you. I thank you, Father, that you have shown me that you will give me that which is good. And now I pray for your continued blessing of strength and for courage. I pray that you continue to remind me that the victory has already been won. I pray that you enable me to continue to grow in faith and in trust in you, for I am weak. I am a coward. I pray that you continue to place in my life those good examples of courage. Again, O Father of all, I thank you for your might. I thank you for your wisdom, and I thank you for your mercy. Amen.

Last night, Wednesday, May 11, 2016, I was at an AA meeting, a meeting which I have chosen to attend on a regular basis primarily because it tends to be more spiritual in nature. It is a discussion meeting which generally centers round topics from two sources, both of which contain daily readings written for the purpose of helping alcoholics live meaningful and joy filled lives.

Our discussion at this particular meeting in part was about discovering the freedom from the buried emotions that had caused us so much pain. It was about feeling the joy and love of God, and the prayer for the day was this: "I pray that I may feel that God is always there to help me." As I listened to my fellow AA members talk about their experiences as they related to this new found freedom, I had a flashback of something I had read about twenty years before.

As I have mentioned before, it wasn't long after I became sober that I reached out to some of my old friends from the past; friends that I had lost contact with over the years. Among those friends were several guys which I had gone to prep-school with. These were guys that joined me on which was to have been our journey into the ministry. One of those friends was Jim Bauman who was now a pastor in suburban Chicago. It was great renewing this and several other friendships with these guys with which I had been so close to in years past. Many of these old friends, actually most of them have been so supportive to me, and continue to be even today.

Well, Jim would send me copies of his church newsletter articles on a regular basis, and occasionally copies of his sermons. One of those newsletter articles dealt with the question of "What occupies the majority of your thoughts?" That question then, and even now, makes me really stop and think. "What occupies the majority of my thoughts?" And that is the question which came to mind last night at that AA meeting as we were discussing the freedom from the burden of buried emotions, and feeling the joy and love of God.

What occupies the majority of your thoughts? Stop and think about it. I mean really stop and think about it! What occupies the majority of your thoughts? If your answer is anything other than God, you are not going to have that freedom from those burdensome emotions. If your answer is anything other than God, you are going to be holding yourself back from the joy and love that God wants you to have to the full.

For me, and most likely for you as well, the things which have most dominated the majority of my thoughts have varied over the years. And as they varied, so did my well-being. I don't remember when I became able to answer that question with God, but this I do know, when I had reached that stage I had been taken to a much better place.

Is this new found place a constant? No. Sometimes the Devil steps in and rears his ugly head. Sometimes the difficulties that the world throws at me take center stage in my mind. Sometimes my emotions take over. But, thank God, only for a little while. Yes, only for a little while because God has shown me the solution. God has shown me who he is, and he has shown me what he has done. Now when I pray that I might feel that God is always there to help me, I know with certainty that he is! That is the difference today. That is the result of all that God has done in my life.

God appointed him (Jesus) to be head over everything....
The fullness of him who fills everything in every way.
Ephesians 1:22-23

Prayer: Lord, occupy my every thought.

Gracious Lord, you fill the heavens and the earth. Now I pray that you fill my every thought. Lord, you fill the universe with your presence. Now let me know that you are present with me also.

Gracious Lord, the Devil is always trying to take your place in my life. The Devil tries to fill my mind with his lies and deception. The Devil tries to use my emotions against me. Gracious Lord, I pray for strength to cast him aside. I pray that you fill my thoughts with you and your gracious will for me. Gracious Lord, I thank you for filling me in every way. Amen.

You know, sometimes we walk through life and just wonder if it is worth it. And you know what else? There are many that decide that it isn't. Yes. The growing number of suicides are proof that many have decided that life is just not worth it. How sad! Well, I have to wonder as to what people are finding to look forward to or to celebrate in this world today. My wife Diane, when referring to the *Golden Years* of getting older, calls them the *Rusty Years*. I live sixty miles west of Chicago and last night, nearly every night, on the news I hear of the horrible crimes that we commit against each other. Two days ago I saw on the news the devastation caused by several tornados as they swept through Oklahoma. Several weeks ago it was earthquakes in Japan, and last week horrible wild fires in Canada. It just seems to go on and on. Many wonder and ask, "Is it worth it?" Yes. What is there to look forward to or to celebrate in this world of ours today?

As I have spent the last six months digging deep into my past for the writing of this book, I have found it to be a reassurance of something that I had already discovered. I discovered long ago, actually for as long ago as I can remember I have known life is worth living. Just think about it. Every time a child is born into this world it is proof that God knows that life is worth living. If it were not, our God of love would not continue to bless us with the gift of children. Just think about it. If life was not worth living; if there was nothing to look forward to for you and for me, or if there was nothing for us to celebrate in this life, why in the world would our Creator and Protector allow things to go on? He would not. You see, God, in his great love, wants only that which is good for us.

When Jack McCullough was arrested and brought to trial for the kidnap and murder of my sister Maria, my sister Pat and I both were led to looking for the good which might come out of it all. As I look back over this seemingly horrible time in my life I clearly can see the hand of a loving God. Can we get caught up in the horror and tragedy of it all? Yes. And I often did. But God was always there giving me that which I needed most. For me what was there to celebrate? In fact what is there to celebrate in the midst of any tragedy?

I want you to think of it this way: When it is dark out and you suddenly turn on the light, the light is so bright that it shocks your eyes doesn't it? And the darker it is, the brighter the light appears to be. But if you close your eyes to the light, the brightness fades to almost the point of disappearing. The same holds true for this life in which we live. Life goes on. The sun shines in the morning, and we can go with it or we can remain in the darkness. The result depends upon you. You can choose to open your eyes or you can choose to keep them closed.

Some have referred to my life as one filled with tragedy. I do not see it that way. Yes. I recognize the tragedy, or the difficulties as they come, and I do not want to diminish their impact in any way for you or for me. But God has so richly blessed me in the midst of them that they seem pale in comparison. God has given me so much over the years. He has given me more than I often even recognized or opened my eyes to, and certainly more than I deserved. God has, and God continues to give me so much to celebrate, and so much to look forward to. And, as a result, today, when the darkness comes I open my eyes to the light and expect to find something good. And then, when I do, I celebrate.

They will celebrate your abundant goodness.
Psalm 145:7

Prayer: Celebrating God's goodness.

O Gracious God, in your great love you give to me all that I need and so much more. In your great love your light shines in my darkest hour and you give me your blessing. In your great love you show me that in spite of this sinful world my life is worth living. I praise you, and I thank you.

O Gracious God, sometimes the darkness of this world in which I live seems overpowering. Sometimes I get caught up in the horror and tragedy of it all. Sometimes I close my eyes to your goodness. Forgive me.

O Gracious God, I have seen you as you come to me with your gifts of blessing just when I need you the most. O Gracious God, in what appears to be my darkest hour you have given to me until my cup runneth over. I thank you.

O Gracious God, now I pray that you enable me to always open my eyes to you. I pray that you enable me to see you as you come to me. I pray that you enable me to grasp your gifts as they come, and I pray that you enable me to celebrate. Yes, O Gracious God, enable me to rejoice and to celebrate. In Christ Jesus. Amen.

I have shared with you some of the darkness which has plagued my life. I have shared with you the worry and the fear, the feeling of helplessness and emptiness, guilt, forgiveness, anger, and revenge. I have shown my struggle with the *what ifs*, and my search for answers. I have discussed anxiety and depression, along with hope and peace. And you may wonder as I did as to what difference does it make? For me, I have found the answers in God. I look to the Book of Isaiah and in the thirtieth chapter I hear, "Woe to the obstinate children, declares the Lord, to those who carry out plans that are not mine." I read these words and I see myself. No wonder I have struggled with so much, and wallowed in the darkness so often! And then I hear the Sovereign Lord, the Holy One, say this, "In repentance and rest is your salvation, in quietness and trust is your strength." And now, as I sit here and see these words, I see, no, it is much more than that. I sense. I feel that quietness that the Lord wants me to have.

But, just as I say that I am in that quiet place, the Devil strives to make it different. Therefore, I need to work at it, with the help of God. I have been caught up in that turmoil and darkness all too often, and it is a place I do not want to be. But through it all my trust in the Lord has grown exceedingly. That is the difference. That is the result of this journey. Now when I read those words showing my obstinate nature, I can say, "Not me!" At least, not now. Instead I repent, and I rest in my salvation. I trust in the Lord, and my turmoil is turned into quiet. That is the result!

Prayer Index